Irish Fiddle Solos

64 Pieces for Violin

By Pete Cooper

Preface

This collection includes many of my favourite Irish fiddle tunes. Some are easy to play, others more challenging. The bowing techniques, ornamentation and other aspects of playing style summarised in the introduction will be familiar to readers of my earlier book, the Complete Irish Fiddle Player, as will source musicians like Julia Clifford, Tommy Peoples, Lucy Farr, John Doherty and Padraig O'Keeffe. Here though, instead of proceeding in 'fiddle method' style from simpler to more complex tunes, we explore regional repertoire and styles. Grouped in sets for performance, the tunes from any one tradition can be of varying levels of difficulty. Less experienced players may find sets 5, 6 and 29, for example, quite approachable, as well as the first reel in set 14 and the second single jig in set 15.

I am indebted as ever to the many traditional fiddlers and other musicians who over the years have shared their music with me, particularly to Lucy Farr who was still playing tunes at home up to the time of her death at the age of ninety. I'd also like to thank readers of the Complete Irish Fiddle Player who've been kind enough to convey their appreciation of that book, and have also added to my knowledge of some of the players featured there. I hope this new collection will help to sustain and deepen your interest in this great music.

Happy fiddling!

Pete Cooper

pete@petecooper.com

Online Audio www.melbay.com/20919BCDEB

1 2 3 4 5 6 7 8 9 0

Exclusive Sales Agent, Mel Bay Publications Inc., Pacific, MO 63069

IRELAND

ED 12734
British Library Cataloguing-in-Publication Data.
A catalogue record for this book is available from the British Library
ISMN M-2201-2233-0

French translation: Agnès Ausseur
German translation: Ute Corleis
Cover design and page layout by www.adamhaystudio.com
Cover illustration by Chris Price
Music setting and page layout by Jack Thompson
Printed in Germany S&Co.7748

IRISH FIDDLE SOLOS

Solos pour le violon traditionnel irlandais / Soli auf der irischen Fiddle

Contents

Introduction 4
The Fiddle in Ireland 4
Airs 4
Dance Tune Structure 4
Dance Tune Types 4
Bowing 5
Ornamentation 5
Modes and Key Signature 6
Chords 6
Further Listening 55
Index of Pieces by Dance Type 56

Sommaire

Introduction 7
Le violon traditionnel (fiddle) en Irlande 7
Les Airs 7
Structure des airs à danser 7
Les types d'airs à danser 7
Les coups d'archet 8
L'ornementation 9
Modes et armures de la clef 9
Les accords 10
Discographie - écoute 55
Index des pièces par types de danses 56

Inhalt

Einleitung 11
Die Fiddle in Irland 11
Airs [Weisen] 11
Die Struktur des Tanzliedes 11
Tanzlied-Typen 11
Die Benutzung des Bogens 12
Verzierungen 13
Kirchentonarten und Vorzeichen 14
Akkorde 14
Hörempfehlungen 55
Werktitel nach Tanztyp 56

The pieces / Les pièces / Die Stücke

(Set and Track No.) (Page No.)

1 *Slow Air/Air lent/Langsame Air*
Lament for O'Donnell 15
2 *Hornpipes*
Julia Clifford's 16
Sean Healy's 16
3 *Double Jigs*
Tom Billy's Favourite 17
The Bank of Turf 17
4 *Slides*
Scully Casey's 18
Dan O'Keeffe's No. 1 19
Dan O'Keeffe's No. 2 19
5 *Slide/Polka*
Nell O'Sullivan's 20
The Gullane Polka 20
6 *Polkas*
Toormore Polka No. 1 21
Toormore Polka No. 2 21
7 *Polkas*
Knocknaboul Polka 22
Ballydesmond Polka No. 3 22
8 *Reels*
Fergal O'Gara 23
Green Fields of Ros Beigh 23
9 *Clare Jigs*
The Humours of Ennistymon 24
Kilfenora Jig 25
The Cliffs of Moher 25
10 *Slow Air/Air lent/Langsame Air*
Lament for Owen Roe O'Neill 26
11 *Reels*
The Porthole of the Kelp 27
Farewell to Miltown 27
12 *Hornpipes*
The Plains of Boyle 28
McGivney's Hornpipe 28
13 *Polkas*
Ballyhoura Mountains 29
Lucy Farr's Polka 29
14 *Two Galway Reels/Deux Reels de Galway/Zwei Galway Reels*
Andy Davy's 30
The Pullet and the Cock 30
15 *Simple Jigs*
Music on the Wind 31
The Lonesome Jig 31
16 *Two Hornpipes/Deux Hornpipes/Zwei Hornpipes*
The Home Brew 32
Galway Bay Hornpipe 32

(Set and Track No.) (Page No.)

17 *Instrumental Air/Air instrumental/Instrumentale Air*
Michael O'Connor 33
18 *Instrumental Air/Air instrumental/Instrumentale Air*
The Princess Royal 34
19 *Instrumental Air/Air instrumental/Instrumentale Air*
Fanny Power 34
20 *Slip Jigs*
The Dusty Miller 35
A Fig for a Kiss 35
21 *Slip Jig/Double Jigs*
O'Farrell's Welcome to Limerick 36
The Wandering Minstrel 37
Donnybrook Fair 37
22 *Double Jigs*
The Coach Road to Sligo 38
The Trip to Sligo 39
Coleman's Cross 39
23 *Sligo Reels*
Martin Wynne's No. 1 40
No. 2 40
No. 3 41
24 *Air* The Coulin 42
25 *Reels in G/Reels en sol/Reels in G*
Swinging on the Gate 42
Over the Moor to Maggie 43
26 *Reels in A minor/Reels en la mineur/Reels in a-Moll*
The Sligo Maid 44
The Star of Munster 45
27 *Reels*
The Christmas Eve 46
Fermoy Lasses 47
Craig's Pipes 47
28 *Co. Donegal Air/Air du comté de Donegal/Air aus der Grafschaft Donegal*
Paddy's Rambles through the Park 48
29 *Donegal Germans/Allemandes (Germans) de Donegal/Germans aus Donegal*
Rósie Bheag Rósie Móire's 49
Francie Mooney's 49
30 *Donegal Reels/Reels de Donegal/Donegal Reels*
Boys of Malin 50
The Gravel Walks 50
Dinkey's Reel 51
31 *Donegal Reels/Reels de Donegal/Donegal Reels*
The Oak Tree 52
The Flogging Reel 53
The Glory Reel 53
32 *Air* Coming Home 54

Introduction

This collection follows a journey, county by county, from the Cork/Kerry border region known as Sliabh Luachra (pronounced *Shlee-av Look-ra*) in the south, up through Clare, Galway and Sligo to Donegal in the north. Leading exponents of each regional style, past and present, are acknowledged in the short texts about the tunes. Serious students of Irish music are encouraged to find recordings of these important musicians and, if possible, hear them live. The CD, however, gives a general indication of tempo, rhythm and style.

The tunes are presented here in 'sets,' for concert performance, rather than individually. This accords with traditional practice in Ireland, where tunes are similarly grouped, both for informal ensemble playing at 'sessions' and at ceilidh (pronounced *kay-lee*) dances. A set usually consists of two or more tunes of the same type (a set of reels, or a set of jigs, etc.), each tune being played three times through (with repeats) before changing to the next.[1]

Although most tunes seem simple on the page, rarely leaving first position, they require an interpretive technique different from that applied to a classical piece. The difference is not only one of playing style - vibrato, for example, is hardly ever employed - but of approach. Traditionally learned by ear, Irish tunes are always performed by heart, notation being used, if at all, more as a map, or *aide-mémoire*, than as a detailed set of instructions. Hornpipes, for example, are conventionally notated with equal quavers, but are in fact played with a triplet swing (see Dance Tune Types), while ornaments like the 'cut' and the 'roll' are usually supplied at the discretion of the individual. To gain real fluency in this, as in any other, traditional fiddle language, and to build a good repertoire, can take from five to seven years of dedicated listening, practice and playing with others.

The Fiddle In Ireland
'Hang the harpers,' Queen Elizabeth I had declared. The fiddle, as the violin is called in Ireland, was adopted by Irish dance musicians during the 1600s, when English colonial rule was extended from a small area around Dublin to the whole country. Amid the wreckage of the old Gaelic social order, with its courtly music for metal-strung harp and voice, the adoption of the modern violin coincided with the emergence of an extraordinary rural dance culture, which flourished throughout the 1700s and beyond. As early as 1674 a foreign visitor, Richard Head, had observed 'in every field a fiddle, and the lasses footing it till they were all of a foam.'

Eighteenth-century Dublin, with its elegant Georgian architecture, was the home of the European art music patronised by the English and Anglo-Irish upper class. The first performance of Handel's *Messiah* was given there in 1742. The Dublin music scene however faced eastwards towards England and the continent. Irish traditional music developed in the countryside, especially in the west, in a social and political chasm between the native peasantry and their colonial rulers. It was here that itinerant dancing masters, working local circuits, taught deportment and country dances, inventing intricate new steps for jigs, hornpipes and reels. It was the solo uilleann (pronounced *ill-yun*) piper, fiddler or flute-player at the rural 'cross-roads dance' who, together with his later descendants, created the vast present-day repertoire of perhaps ten thousand dance tunes.

Airs
Elements of the older instrumental music survived the destruction of the Gaelic schools of the harpers, poets and singers. Composer and harpist Turloch Carolan (1670-1738), a last great exponent of the tradition, was welcomed in the big houses of both protestant and catholic patrons, creating a unique hybrid of the Gaelic and continental, especially the Italian, styles then fashionable. We can only speculate, however, as to how this native tradition, under more favourable conditions, might have incorporated the modern fiddle, and the new dance rhythms. Although the 1798 Belfast Harp Festival could attract only ten harpers, some at least of their instrumental airs were notated and preserved. Twentieth-century musicians like Derek Bell of The Chieftains have brought this repertoire back into circulation.

In Irish-speaking areas like Connemara or Sliabh Luachra, a tradition of *sean-nós* (old style) unaccompanied singing also survived, the songs imbued with the rhythms and metrical patterns of Gaelic speech and poetry. There also exists a parallel English-language song tradition in Ireland. The melodies, or airs, of these songs may be played as instrumental solos. Their finest interpreters are those familiar with their texts.

Dance Tune Structure
Dance tunes, however, form the core of the Irish fiddle repertoire. In each eight-bar section of the tune, referred to as the A-part and the B-part, the music is structured in two-bar phrases, the repeated melodic building blocks of the piece. By ear, you would start by learning the first phrase, and play it by heart, before adding the second. The third and fourth phrases in the sequence are more quickly grasped, since they usually repeat the opening material, with a modified ending. Play the whole A-part several times through by heart, giving particular attention to how the phrases are connected, before applying the same procedure to learning the B-part.

The aesthetic of Irish dance music is based on creative repetition. The tune does not build slowly to a grand climax like a Romantic piece, but always returns to its own beginning, like the symbols on a rotating prayer-wheel. The ego-anxiety of the player, even the self-expressive urge of the artist, may be relaxed. Conscious use of dynamics is rare. More important in any dance music, whether or not actually played for dancing, is a contrast between accented and weak notes.

Dance Tune Types
Note: The tempo indications here refer to playing for dancing. Many musicians play more slowly. A steady pulse and correct distribution of accents are always more important than metronomic 'correctness.'

The **Reel** is played briskly in 'cut' time, with two minim beats to a bar, (𝅗𝅥 = c.112/120). Subtle shifts of accent between the down-beat and the off-beat may be explored by more experienced players. Reels with a total of only 16 bars, instead of the usual 32, are called *single reels*.

Jigs are of three kinds, the *double jig* (♩. = c.126) is in 6/8; the *slip-jig* (♩. = c.144) in 9/8; and the *single jig* or *slide*, particularly associated with Cork and Kerry, (♩. = 132-138) in 12/8 time. The characteristic 'lilt' of a double jig, with its two beats to a bar, is produced by lengthening the first quaver at the expense of the second.

Example 1

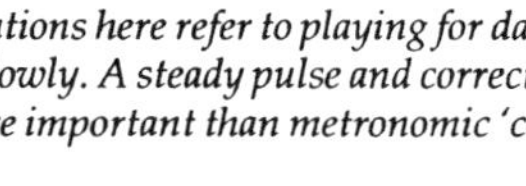

Though slower than reels, **hornpipes** are also in cut time (𝅗𝅥 = c.92). They are played, not as written but with a triplet swing, i.e. with the first of each pair of quavers twice as long as the second.

Example 2

The nineteenth-century, pan-European **polka** is usually played fast in Cork and Kerry (♩ = c. 132-138) in 2/4 time, often with a stressed off-beat.

1 *For reasons of space, tunes are played only a rather hectic once or twice on the CD*

A type of *barndance* associated particularly with Donegal, the **german** (short for 'German schottische') is played (𝅗𝅥 = c. 106) in cut time, either 'straight' as written, or with the triplet swing of a hornpipe.

Bowing

Except in the case of slow airs, Irish players tend to use no more than a fifth of the length of the bow, often very much less, and usually at a point around two-thirds of the way up the stick. An alternation between successive moments of lightness and weight lies at the heart of good dance-style bowing technique. The player must always feel the beat, and foot-tapping is not unusual. Slurs are marked in this edition, along with optional, 'dotted' slurs for the more ambitious. Newcomers should find these useful, though experienced Irish-style fiddlers will feel free to supply both bowing and ornaments according to taste. The bow remains mostly on the string and a variety of bowing patterns articulate the rhythm, depending on tune type. Many players like to use a down-bow for the very last note of a tune. Bear in mind that notation describes only the horizontal direction of the bow, not its 'vertical' dimension, which must be felt.

In general, accents are of two kinds. What I call *hard* accents are produced by the attack at the start of a new bow-stroke (either up or down) and will be familiar to most violinists. Instead of deliberately 'pressing down,' however, just feel your arm-weight in the wrist and hand. The forearm and wrist are like a dancer, in a continual state of play with the force of gravity. *Soft* accents are made by an increase of bow-speed and arm-weight in *mid-stroke,* leaning into the second of two slurred notes, or the middle note of three. Begin the bow-stroke lightly, then bring arm-weight to bear on the strong note.

Jigs, for example, have two accented notes to a bar, the first of each triplet. A one-note-to a-bow pattern produces an alternation of down- and up-strokes (*hard* accents) on the beat. When this pattern is disrupted by a crotchet, 'normality' can be restored with a slur onto the next accented beat, a *soft* accent.

Example 3: Tom Billy's Favourite

The *Wandering Minstrel* can be bowed entirely in this basic pattern. You may also try the optional (dotted) slurs in the C-part, introducing more soft accents in a pattern that resolves itself over four bars.

Example 4: Wandering Minstrel

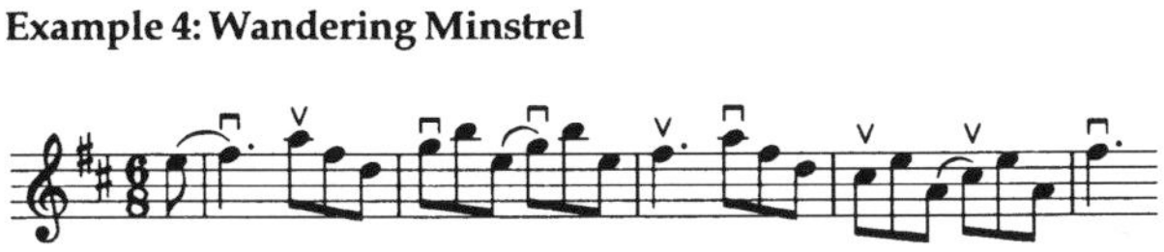

A useful bowing pattern for **reels** and **hornpipes**, also with their two-to-a-bar beat, is what I call 3-3-2 bowing. In a typical bar of eight quavers the first three are bowed singly, the next three slurred, the last two bowed singly again:

Example 5: Over the Moor to Maggie

As in jigs, this produces an alternation of down-bow and up-bow accents on the beat, though in this case the first accent is hard, while the second, which falls on the middle note of the slurred three, is soft. Another useful pattern for reels is one-down-three-up bowing, often used with a 'cut' to separate two notes of the same pitch:

Example 6: Andy Davy's, B1

The next example, from a hornpipe, uses three other common bowing techniques: (i) a slur out of a triplet; (ii) *cross-bowing*, where the slurs lie across the beat; and (iii) a single down-stroke between two up-bow slurs, which brings out a strong off-beat accent:

Example 7: Home Brew

Polkas are generally played with two bow-strokes to a bar, with the (soft) accent often being felt on the off-beat, even on a dotted quaver, where this is not apparent from the notation.

Example 8: Gullane Polka

Some fiddlers consider that in **reels** too the off-beat accent is more important than the down-beat. In either case the art is to establish an expectation in the listener's mind, then subtly to subvert it, perhaps with a change of bowing or ornamentation. The *roll*, for example, tends to accentuate the off-beat.

Ornamentation

How you ornament, or bow, or vary the melody of the tune is part of your individual art. The written indication of specific ornaments (as here) would be regarded by experienced traditional players as over-prescriptive and many decorations are interchangeable. Flutes, whistles, uilleann pipes and other instruments all have equivalents of the fiddle ornaments. Intricate piping decoration, for example, is reproduced by some fiddlers. In general, ornamentation serves a *rhythmic* function.

The *roll*, like the classical *turn*, consists of five notes always slurred in one stroke, in wave form: the principal note, a note above it, the principal note again, the note below it, then the principal note once more. When the principal note is played with the *first* finger, it's usually the *third*, not the second finger, that plays the upper note.

Example 9: First, second and third-finger rolls

As well as rolls on first, second or third-finger principal notes, an *open-string roll* can also be used. Here is an example from a jig.

Example 10: The Bank of Turf

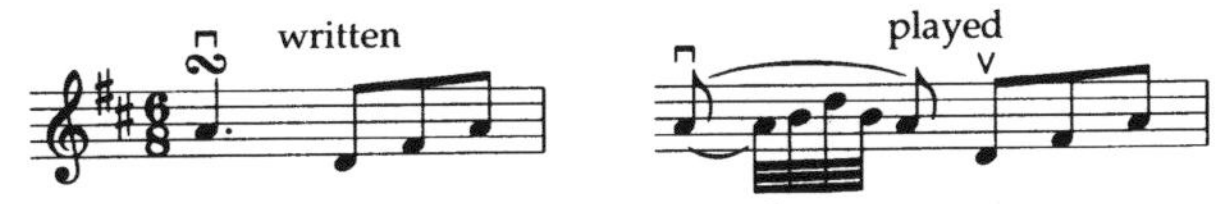

Unlike the turn, the roll requires the use of a subtle but strong bow accent on the *off-beat* to produce its almost percussive effect. The precise timing of the accent *within* the cluster of five notes depends on whether the principle note is a dotted crotchet falling on the beat, in which case it is played as a ***long roll***.

Example 11: Porthole of the Kelp

Or the roll may be indicated above a crotchet that is already, as it were, on the off-beat, albeit preceded by a tied quaver. In this case it's as if the bow-accent triggers the so-called short roll:

Example 12: Green Fields of Ros Beigh

The ***slide*** is a left-hand *portamento* rising to the notated pitch from a quarter- or semi-tone below it. It is routinely used to accentuate an important note.

Example 13: Coach Road to Sligo

In this collection it is indicated (with a diagonal /) only on longer notes. A ***cut*** is a light flick of a finger across the string, generally to accentuate a note, and often in conjunction with *one-down-three-up* bowing pattern to articulate two slurred notes of the same pitch. The third finger is usually used to ornament a first-finger note.

Example 14: Fergal O'Gara

The percussive bow-driven ***treble***, or *shiver*, or in Scottish parlance, *shoogle*, has no equivalent in classical violin. The three notes are not 'bowed,' even quickly, in the normal way, with three separate strokes. Instead, a rapid stuttering of the bow is produced with a jerk of the wrist or arm. It is not uncommon to slur out of the last note of the treble (as out of a triplet, example 7) to the next melody note.

Example 15: The Gravel Walks, B-part

In this case the treble occurs on a down-beat. It can also be used, like the *roll*, to impart on off-beat accent. Some players prefer a down-bow treble, others an up-bow treble. The latter is often preceded by two quavers slurred on a down-bow.

Example 16: The Flogging Reel

The C-part of *The Oak Tree* uses up- and down-bow trebles alternately.

Example 17: The Oak Tree

A similar bow shake occurs in some jigs.

Example 18: Trip to Sligo B4/5

Open-string drones, as well as double stops, are also sometimes used.

Modes and Key Signatures

As a basis for their tune-making, early rural fiddlers used 'modal' scales, already archaic in the art music of the period, but perhaps allowing them to draw upon elements of the older Gaelic music. The practice has continued ever since. Consider the three reels in Set 30. All are 'in A,' but the first, *Boys of Malin*, is in the Ionian (= major) mode of A, the third, *Dinkey's*, is in the Mixolydian (major third, flattened 7th), while the *Gravel Walks* is in the Dorian (minor 3rd, major 6th). A fourth mode, the Aeolian (minor 3rd, minor 6th), is also encountered in Irish music (e.g. the *Fermoy Lasses*), but less often.

The key signatures here are not based on the diatonic major/ minor system, but follow 'folk' convention: sharps or flats that do not actually occur in the tune are not given. A key signature of two sharps may thus indicate D-Ionian, A- Mixolydian, E-Dorian or, in theory, B-Aeolian, depending on which mode corresponds to the final note. For ease of use, each tune's mode is stated here, though one quickly learns to sense the 'tonic' or 'final' to which the tune (usually) comes 'home.' For tunes in the (Ionian) major keys, only the letter name is given. Irish tunes in E and B are almost invariably in the 'minor'-sounding Dorian or Aeolian modes. Some tunes, e.g. *Andy Davy's*, are based on a pentatonic scale, while others combine modes, or alternate between them from one part of the tune to another. The third degree of the scale may be entirely absent, as in *Dan O'Keeffe's No. 1* and *Tom Billy's Favourite*.

Many older rural players pitch certain notes of the scale, the third and sixth especially, as quarter-tones between the natural and the sharp. Such 'lonesome' notes, which may sound 'out of tune' to anyone familiar only with equal temperament, are indicated with an arrow (↑ or ↓) above the stave, and are a valuable expressive resource.

Chords

The old tradition of solo performance has evolved into an ensemble tradition of playing in approximate, 'heterophonous,' unison, with fiddles, whistles, flutes, concertinas, uilleann pipes and button accordions all playing the same melody, *more or less*. Only with band arrangements including piano, guitar and, since the 1960s, an Irish version of the Greek bouzouki, has the question arisen as to what chords to use. While this has not been answered with any degree of unanimity, traditional music has benefited from the enrichment of harmonic possibilities in twentieth-century art music. The chords indicated here, by letter names above the stave, are merely suggestions. They work best as 'open' chords that do not over-define the major or minor third.

Introduction

Ce recueil suit un parcours menant, comté par comté, de la région des confins de Cork et Kerry, appelée Sliabh Luachra, au sud à Donegal dans le nord, en passant par Clare, Galway et Sligo. Les principales personnalités, passées et présentes, illustrant chaque style régional sont présentées dans des textes brefs en tête des différents airs. Pour étudier sérieusement la musique irlandaise, les néophytes sont fortement incités à se procurer des enregistrements effectués par ces éminents musiciens et, si possible, à les écouter en direct. Le CD d'accompagnement donne toutefois des indications générales de tempo, de rythme et de style.

Les airs sont regroupés ici en séries (*sets*) destinées au concert, conformément à la pratique traditionnelle irlandaise qui rassemble des airs similaires tant lors des *sessions* d'ensemble informelles qu'au cours des danses *ceilidh*. Un *set* est généralement constitué d'au moins deux airs du même genre (série de *reels*, série de gigues, etc.), chaque air étant joué trois fois, avec ses reprises, avant de passer au suivant.[1]

Malgré l'apparence facile de la plupart des airs, quittant rarement la première position, ceux-ci exigent une démarche d'interprétation différente de celle requise par une pièce pour violon classique, non seulement dans la technique de jeu – le vibrato, par exemple, n'est pratiquement jamais employé – mais également dans l'approche. Appris à l'oreille, selon la tradition, les airs irlandais sont donc toujours exécutés par cœur ; la notation, quand elle existe, sert d'aide-mémoire plus qu'elle ne fournit d'indications précises. Ainsi, par exemple, les *hornpipes* sont-ils notés, conventionnellement, en croches égales alors qu'ils sont, en fait, joués selon une pulsation ternaire (voir Les types d'airs à danser), et les ornements comme le *cut* ou le *roll* sont-ils laissés au choix de chaque interprète. Obtenir une réelle aisance dans ce langage du violon traditionnel irlandais, comme dans tout autre, et s'y constituer un solide répertoire peuvent prendre de cinq à sept années d'écoute concentrée, de pratique suivie et d'exécution d'ensemble régulière.

Le violon traditionnel (*fiddle*) en Irlande

« Pendez les harpistes » proclamait la reine Elizabeth Ière. Le *fiddle*, nom donné au violon en Irlande, fut adopté par les musiciens de danse irlandais au cours des années 1600, alors que la domination coloniale anglaise s'étendit des alentours de Dublin au pays en entier. Au milieu de l'anéantissement du vieil ordre social gaélique, et de sa musique de cour pour la harpe à cordes de métal et voix, le ralliement au violon moderne coïncida avec l'émergence d'une culture de danse paysanne extraordinaire qui s'épanouit bien au-delà des années 1700. Dès 1674, un visiteur étranger, Richard Head, observait : « dans tous les champs joue un violon au son duquel les jeunes filles dansent à en être tout écumantes. »

Le Dublin du XVIIIème siècle, avec son élégante architecture georgienne, était le foyer de l'art musical européen soutenu par la classe dirigeante anglaise et anglo-irlandaise. La création du *Messiah* de Haendel s'y déroula en 1742. Cependant, alors que la scène musicale de Dublin avait les yeux tournés vers l'est, vers l'Angleterre et le continent, la musique traditionnelle irlandaise se développa dans les campagnes, en particulier à l'ouest du pays, dans un climat de clivage social et politique séparant les paysans originaires du crû et les dirigeants coloniaux. C'est là que les maîtres de danse itinérants, se déplaçant en circuits locaux, enseignèrent les postures et les danses paysannes et inventèrent de nouveaux pas complexes pour les gigues, les *hornpipes* et les *reels*. Ce sont les joueurs de fifre, les violonistes, les flûtistes *uilleann* (pronocer *il-youn*) solistes et leurs descendants qui créèrent, lors des *cross-roads dances* (bals) campagnards, le vaste répertoire actuel riche de quelques dix mille airs de danses.

[1] *Du fait de l'espace limité, les airs ne sont joués qu'une ou deux fois rapides sur le CD.*

Les Airs

Quelques éléments de l'ancienne musique instrumentale survécurent à la destruction des écoles gaéliques de harpistes, de poètes et de chanteurs. Le compositeur et harpiste Turloch Carolan (1670-1738), l'un des derniers grands représentants de cette tradition, était accueilli dans les grandes maisons de mécènes tant catholiques que protestants et créa un style unique, hybride des styles gaéliques et continentaux, surtout italiens, alors en vogue. On ne peut toutefois qu'imaginer comment cette tradition autochtone, dans des conditions plus favorables, aurait pu intégrer le *fiddle* moderne et les nouveaux rythmes de danses. Bien que le Festival de harpe de Belfast de 1738 n'eût réuni que dix harpistes, certains, au moins, de leurs airs instrumentaux furent transcrits et préservés. Les musiciens du XXème siècle comme Derek Bell et The Chieftains ont remis ce répertoire en circulation.

Dans les régions de langue irlandaise, comme le Connemara ou Sliabh Luachra, survécut également une tradition de chant non-accompagné *sean-nos* (style ancien) imprégné des rythmes et des formules métriques de la prose et de la poésie gaéliques. Il existe aussi, et parallèlement, une tradition de chant de langue anglaise en Irlande. Les mélodies, ou *airs*, de ces chants peuvent être jouées en solos instrumentaux ; leurs meilleurs interprètes se révèlent, toutefois, être ceux qui connaissent le mieux les textes des *airs*.

Structure des airs à danser

Les airs à danser forment, néanmoins, le cœur du répertoire du *fiddle* irlandais. Dans chacune des sections de huit mesures de l'air, désignées partie A et partie B, la musique est construite par phrases de deux mesures qui constituent les soubassements mélodiques répétés de chaque pièce. On commence par apprendre, à l'oreille, la première phrase puis la jouer par cœur avant d'y ajouter la deuxième. Les troisièmes et quatrièmes phrases de la séquence sont plus faciles à saisir puisqu'elles reprennent généralement les toutes premières mesures avec une fin différente. Jouez la partie A entièrement plusieurs fois par cœur, en concentrant spécialement votre attention sur la façon dont les phrases sont reliées, avant de réitérer la même démarche pour l'apprentissage de la partie B.

L'esthétique de la musique de danse irlandaise s'appuie sur la répétition créatrice. L'air ne s'achemine pas lentement vers son apogée, comme une pièce romantique, mais revient toujours à son propre début, comme les symboles d'un moulin à prière en rotation. L'angoisse personnelle de l'interprète ou le besoin impérieux de l'artiste de s'exprimer s'en trouvent relâchés. L'emploi conscient de nuances dynamiques est rare. Dans toute musique de danse, qu'elle soit jouée pour être dansée ou non, une valeur primordiale est accordée au contraste entre notes accentuées et notes faibles.

Les types d'airs à danser

N.B. : les indications de tempo se rattachent ici à l'accompagnement de la danse. Beaucoup de musiciens jouent plus lentement. Une pulsation régulière et la distribution juste des accentuations prendront toujours le pas sur l'exactitude métronomique.

Le ***reel*** se joue rapidement sur un rythme « coupé » (*cut*) comportant deux blanches par mesure (𝅗𝅥 = *ca* 112/120). Des déplacement subtils d'accents entre le temps faible et le temps fort pourront être exploités par des interprètes plus avancés. Les *reels* comportant 16 mesures, au lieu des 32 habituelles, sont appelés *single reels* (*reels* simples)

Les ***Jigs*** **(gigues)** sont de trois sortes : *double jig* (♩. = *ca* 126) à 6/8, *slip-jig* (♩. = *ca* 144) à 9/8 et *single jig* ou *slide*, particulièrement associée à Cork et Kerry, (♩. = 132-138) à 12/8. Le « balancement » caractéristique de la double gigue, à deux temps par mesure, est obtenu par l'allongement de la première croche au détriment de la deuxième.

Exemple 1

Bien que plus lents que les *reels*, les ***hornpipes*** sont également mesurés à 2/2 (𝅗𝅥 = *ca* 92). Ils sont joués non pas conformément à leur notation mais selon une pulsation ternaire, c'est-à-dire que la durée de la première de chaque paire de croches est deux fois plus longue que celle de la deuxième.

Exemple 2

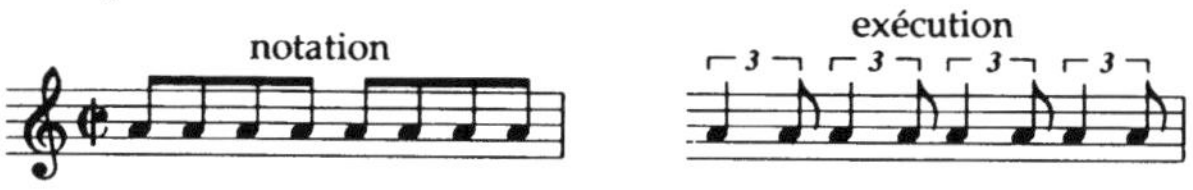

La très européenne ***polka*** du XIXe siècle, est en général jouée vite dans les régions de Cork et de Kerry (♩ = *ca* 132-138) à 2/4, avec un accent fréquent sur le temps faible)

Un genre de *barndance* associée en particulier à la région de Donegal, la ***german*** (abréviation de *German schottische* [écossaise allemande]) est joué à 2/2 (𝅗𝅥 = *ca* 106) soit en respectant exactement la notation, soit avec la pulsation ternaire du *hornpipe*.

Les coups d'archet

Sauf dans les airs lents, les musiciens irlandais ont tendance à n'utiliser qu'un cinquième de la longueur de l'archet, souvent beaucoup moins, et généralement à un point situé à environ aux deux tiers de la baguette vers la hausse. L'alternance d'épisodes successifs légers et pesants se trouve au cœur de la technique de coup d'archet du style dansé. L'interprète se doit de toujours ressentir la pulsation et la marquer du pied n'est pas inhabituel. Dans cette édition, des liaisons de phrasé utiles aux débutants sont indiquées, ainsi que des liaisons de phrasé optionnelles en pointillé destinées aux interprètes plus ambitieux. Les violonistes irlandais traditionnels expérimentés seront libres d'adapter les coups d'archet et l'ornementation à leur goût. L'archet est maintenu la plupart du temps sur la corde et diverses formules de coups d'archet articulent le rythme en fonction du type d'air. De nombreux interprètes affectionnent le tiré sur la toute dernière note d'un air. N'oubliez pas que la notation ne décrit que la direction horizontale de l'archet et pas sa dimension « verticale » qu'il faut savoir apprécier.

En général, les accents sont de deux sortes. Ce que j'appelle les accents « durs », familiers à la plupart des violonistes, sont produits à l'attaque au début d'un nouveau coup d'archet (tiré ou poussé). Toutefois, au lieu «d'appuyer» volontairement, efforcez-vous de porter le poids du bras dans le poignet et la main. L'avant-bras et le poignet sont, comme un danseur, en continuel état d'équilibre avec la force de gravité. Les accents « doux » sont obtenus par l'accélération de la vitesse de l'archet et l'augmentation du poids du bras à mi-course du coup d'archet, s'appuyant sur la deuxième de deux notes legato ou sur la note du milieu d'un groupe de trois. Attaquez le coup d'archet légèrement, puis portez le poids du bras sur la note accentuée.

Les ***jigs*** (gigues), par exemple, comportent deux notes accentuées par mesure, la première de chaque triolet. La formule appliquant « une note par coup d'archet » provoque l'alternance de tirés et de poussés (accents durs) sur les temps. Si cette formule est interrompue par une noire, la « normalité » sera restaurée par une liaison de phrasé vers le temps suivant accentué d'un accent doux.

Exemple 3 : Tom Billy's Favourite

Wandering Minstrel peut être phrasé entièrement selon cette formule de base dans laquelle on pourra également expérimenter l'option offerte par les liaisons de phrasé en pointillé dans la partie C, introduisant ainsi plus d'accents doux dans une configuration déployée sur quatre mesures.

Exemple 4 : Wandering Minstrel

Dans les *reels* et les *hornpipes*, la formule de coup d'archet que j'appelle « 3-3-2 », peut s'appliquer utilement, y compris dans les mesures à deux pulsations. Elle consiste, dans une mesure comportant huit croches, à donner un coup d'archet sur les trois premières croches, à lier les trois suivantes et redonner un coup d'archet sur les deux dernières :

Exemple 5 : Over the Moor to Maggie

Comme dans les gigues, ceci provoque une alternance d'accents poussés et tirés sur le temps, quoique, en l'occurrence, le premier accent soit dur, tandis que le deuxième, qui tombe sur la note centrale des trois notes liées, est doux.

Une autre formule utilisée dans les *reels* est celle du coup d'archet « un tiré, trois poussés », faisant souvent intervenir une « coupure » pour séparer deux notes de même hauteur :

Exemple 6 : Andy Davy's, B1

L'exemple suivant, tiré d'un *hornpipe*, développe trois autres techniques courantes de coups d'archet : (i) la liaison d'un triolet à une autre note, (ii) le « coup d'archet croisé » (*cross-bowing)* dans lequel les liaisons s'étirent sur tout le temps et (iii) un tiré isolé placé entre deux poussés qui fait ressortir un accent fort sur le contretemps :

Exemple 7 : Home Brew

Les **polkas** sont en général jouées avec deux coups d'archet par mesure, l'accent doux étant souvent placé à contretemps même sur une croche pointée, ce que la notation n'indique pas.

Exemple 8 : Gullane Polka

Certains violonistes considèrent que dans les *reels* également l'accentuation à contretemps est plus importante que le temps fort. Dans tous les cas, l'art consiste à créer une attente chez l'auditeur, puis de la détourner avec subtilité, à l'aide d'un changement de coup d'archet ou d'un ornement. Le *roll*, par exemple, accentue le contretemps.

L'ornementation

Les manières d'orner la mélodie d'un air, d'y placer les coups d'archet ou de la varier sont les éléments constitutifs de l'art de chacun. Les notations d'ornements spécifiques (comme ici) paraîtront trop dirigistes aux violonistes traditionnels chevronnés et beaucoup des figurations sont interchangeables. Les flûtes, les sifflets, les fifres *uilleann*, entre autres instruments, pratiquent tous des ornements équivalents à ceux du *fiddle*. Ainsi, par exemple, les figurations complexes du fifre sont-elles reproduites par certains violonistes. En règle générale, l'ornementation sert un propos essentiellement *rythmique*.

Le ***roll***, comme le *turn* (*grupetto)* classique, est formé de cinq notes toujours liées en un seul coup d'archet en forme de vague : note principale, note supérieure, note principale, note inférieure et retour à la note principale. Si la note principale est attaquée par l'index, c'est généralement l'annulaire, et non le majeur, qui joue la note supérieure.

Exemple 9 : *rolls* du premier, deuxième et troisième doigts

De même que le *roll* de la note principale par l'index, le majeur et l'annulaire, on peut aussi exécuter un *roll* sur les cordes à vide, comme dans l'exemple suivant extrait d'une gigue :

Exemple 10 : The Bank of Turf

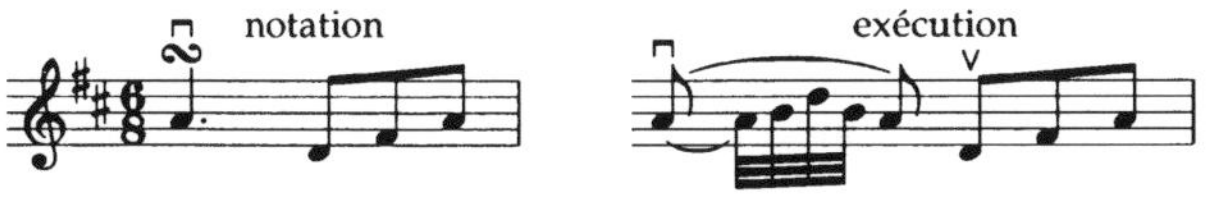

Contrairement au *grupetto*, le *roll* suppose un coup d'archet subtil et fort sur le contretemps pour produire un effet presque percutant. La précision de l'intervention de l'accent à l'intérieur du groupe de cinq notes dépend de la nature de la note principale. Si c'est une noire pointée tombant sur le temps fort, on exécute un ***long roll*** (*roll* long).

Exemple 11 : Porthole of the Kelp

Si le *roll* est indiqué au-dessus d'une noire déjà placée sur le contretemps, même précédée d'une croche liée, le coup d'archet accentué entraîne alors un ***short roll*** (*roll* court) :

Exemple 12 : Green Fields of Ros Beigh

Le ***slide*** est un *portamento* de la main gauche qui atteint la hauteur de la note écrite depuis le quart de ton ou le demi-ton inférieur. Il est communément employé pour mettre en valeur une note importante.

Exemple 13 : Coach Road to Sligo

Dans ce recueil, le *slide* n'est indiqué (par un signe diagonal /) que pour les notes longues.

Le *cut* est un léger claquement du doigt sur la corde, effectué en général pour accentuer une note et associé à la formule de coup d'archet « un tiré, trois poussés » de façon à phraser deux notes liées de même hauteur. On orne habituellement une note jouée à l'index par l'annulaire.

Exemple 14 : Fergal O'Gara

Le ***treble*** ou ***shiver*** percutant mené de l'archet, appelé ***shoogle*** en langue écossaise, n'a pas d'équivalent dans la technique de violon classique. Les trois notes ne sont pas « phrasées » avec trois coups d'archet séparés habituels, même rapides. Un battement rapide de l'archet est obtenu par le tressautement du poignet ou du bras. Il arrive couramment de lier la dernière note du *treble* à la note suivante de la mélodie (à l'image de la liaison du triolet, exemple 7).

Exemple 15 : The Gravel Walks, partie B

Dans ce cas, le *treble* se place à contretemps. On peut aussi l'employer, comme le *roll*, pour accentuer le contretemps. Certains interprètes favorisent le *treble* poussé, d'autres le *treble* tiré, ce dernier étant souvent précédé de deux croches liées sur un tiré.

Exemple 16 : The Flogging Reel

La partie C de *The Oak Tree* alterne les *treble* tirés et poussés.

Exemple 17 : The Oak Tree

On rencontre un tremblement similaire de l'archet dans certaines gigues.

Exemple 18 : Trip to Sligo, mes.4/5

On a également parfois recours au bourdon sur corde à vide ainsi qu'aux doubles cordes.

Modes et armures de la clef

Les premiers violonistes traditionnels campagnards ont eu recours, comme cadre fondamental de leur musique, à des échelles modales déjà archaïques dans l'art musical de leur époque mais qui leur permirent de se servir d'éléments propres à l'ancienne musique gaélique. La pratique s'en est perpétuée depuis. Si l'on considère les trois *reels* constituant la série 30, tous sont en *la*, le premier, *Boys of Malin*, est en mode ionien (=majeur), le troisième, *Dinkey's*, est en mode mixolydien (tierce majeure, septième mineure) et *The Gravel Walks* est en mode dorien (tierce mineure sixte majeure). On rencontre aussi le mode éolien (tierce mineure, sixte mineure) dans la musique irlandaise, mais beaucoup moins fréquemment (*Fermoy Lasses*, par exemple).

L'armure de la clef n'est pas gouvernée ici par le système diatonique majeur/mineur, mais suit la convention traditionnelle qui veut que les dièses ou les bémols qui n'apparaissent pas effectivement dans la pièce ne soient pas indiqués. Une armure de deux dièses à la clef peut donc signifier *ré* ionien, *la* mixolydien, *mi* dorien ou, théoriquement, *si* éolien, en fonction du mode qui correspond à la note finale. Le mode est indiqué en tête de chaque pièce pour en faciliter l'apprentissage. On apprendra vite, toutefois, à ressentir la « tonique » ou « note finale » par laquelle se termine (généralement) un air. Seule la tonique est donnée pour les airs en mode majeur (ionien). Les airs irlandais en *mi* et en *si* sont presque invariablement dans les modes dorien ou éolien, proches à l'oreille du mode mineur. Certains airs, par exemple *Andy Davy's*, sont construits sur une échelle pentatonique, tandis que d'autres combinent les modes ou les alternent d'une partie de l'air à l'autre. Le troisième degré de la gamme peut être totalement absent, comme dans *Dan O'Keeffe's* No1 et *Tom Billy's Favourite*.

Beaucoup d'interprètes campagnards plus âgés accordent certains degrés de l'échelle, en particulier le troisième et le sixième, un quart de ton entre la note naturelle et la note diésée. Ces notes « solitaires », qui peuvent paraître « fausses » aux oreilles habituées au seul tempérament égal, sont signalées par une flèche (↑ou ↓) placée au-dessus de la portée et représentent une ressource expressive de grande valeur.

Les accords

L'ancienne tradition de jeu soliste a évolué vers une tradition de formations jouant à l'unisson « hétérophone » approximatif et comportant *fiddles*, sifflets, flûtes, concertinas, fifres *uilleann* et accordéons à boutons qui exécutent tous, plus ou moins, la même mélodie. Ce n'est qu'avec l'arrangement pour l'ensemble formé d'un piano, d'une guitare et, depuis les années 1960, d'une version irlandaise du *bouzouki* grec qu'a surgi la question de savoir quels accords utiliser. Bien que cette évolution n'ait pas fait l'unanimité, la musique traditionnelle savante a bénéficié de l'enrichissement apporté par l'harmonie au cours du XXème siècle. Les accords indiqués ici par des lettres au-dessus de la portée ne constituent que de simples suggestions et sonnent mieux sous leur forme « ouverte » qui n'insiste par sur la définition majeure ou mineure de la tierce.

Einleitung

Diese Sammlung wandelt auf den Spuren einer Reise durch die Grafschaften, die in der südlichen Grenzregion Cork/Kerry, bekannt unter dem Namen Sliabh Luachra (ausgeprochen als *Schlie-af Luck-ra*) beginnt und durch Clare, Galway sowie Sligo bis hinauf nach Donegal im Norden führt. Bedeutende Interpreten des jeweiligen Stils einer Region, sowohl aus früherer als auch heutiger Zeit, werden in den kurzen Texten über die Lieder angegeben. Bei einem ernsthaften Studium der irischen Musik sollte man sich bemühen, Aufnahmen von diesen wichtigen Musikern zu bekommen oder - noch besser - sie sich live anzuhören. Die beigefügte CD wiederum gibt allgemeine Hinweise zu Tempo, Rhythmus und Stil.

Die Melodien werden hier nicht individuell dargestellt, sondern in ‚Gruppen', so dass sie für Konzertaufführungen geeignet sind. Diese Vorgehensweise stimmt mit der traditionellen Praxis in Irland überein, wo Lieder auf ähnliche Weise sowohl beim zwanglosen Ensemblespiel, den ‚Sessions', als auch bei Ceilidh-Tänzen (ausgesprochen als *kei-lie*) zusammengestellt werden. Eine Gruppe besteht normalerweise aus zwei oder mehr Liedern desselben Typus (eine Gruppe mit Reels, Jigs, usw.), wobei jede Melodie dreimal (mit Wiederholungen) durchgespielt wird bevor man zur nächsten wechselt.[1]

Obwohl die meisten Lieder auf dem Notenpapier einfach aussehen und nur selten die erste Lage verlassen, erfordern sie eine Interpretationstechnik, die sich von der unterscheidet, die man bei klassischen Stücken anwendet. Der Unterschied macht sich nicht nur in der Art zu Spielen bemerkbar – Vibrato wird zum Beispiel fast nie angewendet –, sondern vor allem in der Herangehensweise. Traditionell werden die irischen Lieder über das Hören gelernt. Daher werden sie immer auswendig gespielt und wenn Notation überhaupt verwendet wird, dann mehr als eine Art Orientierungshilfe oder Gedächtnisstütze denn als ausführliche Interpretationsanweisung. Hornpipes zum Beispiel werden üblicherweise in gleichlangen Achtelnoten aufgeschrieben, tatsächlich aber eher triolisch gespielt (s. auch den Abschnitt Tanzlied-Typen). Verzierungen wie der ‚Cut' und der ‚Roll' wiederum werden dem Ermessen jedes Einzelnen überlassen.

Wie bei jeder anderen traditionell überlieferten Fiddle-Sprache auch kann es zwischen 5 und 7 Jahren dauern, die man mit intensivem Hören, Üben und Spielen verbringt, bis man in ihr eine echte Gewandtheit erzielt und ein gutes Repertoire aufgebaut hat.

Die Fiddle in Irland

‚Hang the harpers' (‚Hängt die Harfenisten auf') hatte Königin Elizabeth I verkündet. Die Fiddle, wie die Violine in Irland genannt wird, wurde von irischen Tanzmusikern im 16. Jahrhundert übernommen. Damals breitete sich die englische Kolonialmacht von einem kleinen Gebiet um Dublin herum über das ganze Land aus. Inmitten der Trümmer der alten gälischen Sozialordnung mit ihrer höfischen Musik für metallbesaitete Harfe und Stimme traf die Übernahme der modernen Violine auf das Entstehen einer außergewöhnlichen ländlichen Tanzkultur, die das ganze 17. Jahrhundert hindurch und darüber hinaus blühte. Bereits im Jahre 1674 hatte ein ausländische Besucher, Richard Head, beobachtet, dass 'in every field a fiddle, and the lasses footing it till they were all of a foam' („auf jedem Feld gab es eine Fiddle und die Mädchen tanzten dazu, bis sie völlig erschöpft waren".)

Das Dublin des 18. Jahrhunderts mit seiner eleganten georgianischen Architektur war die Heimat der europäischen Kunstmusik, die von der englischen und anglo-irischen Oberschicht gefördert wurde. Hier war die Uraufführung von Händels *Messias* im Jahre 1742. Dennoch blickte die Musikszene von Dublin ostwärts, nämlich nach England und zum Festland. Auf dem Land, und besonders im Westen, entwickelte sich die traditionelle irische Musik in einer gesellschaftlichen und politischen Kluft zwischen der einheimischen Bauernschaft und ihren kolonialen Machthabern. Es war in diesem Umfeld, dass umherziehende Tanzlehrer, die ihre auf ein bestimmtes Gebiet festgelegten Rundreisen absolvierten, die Körperhaltung und englische Volkstänze lehrten, wobei sie komplizierte neue Schritte für Jigs, Hornpipes und Reels erfanden. Es war der solistische Uilleann-Dudelsackspieler (ausgesprochen *ill-jann*), Fiedler oder Flötenspieler beim ländlichen ‚cross-roads dance', der zusammen mit seinen Nachfolgern das gewaltige, vielleicht zehntausend Tanzlieder umfassende Repertoire von heute schuf.

Airs [Weisen]

Einige Elemente der älteren Instrumentalmusik überlebten die Zerstörung der gälischen Harfen-, Dicht- und Gesangsschulen. Der Komponist und Harfenist Turloch Carolan (1670 – 1738), einer der letzten großen Vertreter dieser Tradition, wurde in den großen Häusern sowohl der protestantischen als auch der katholischen Förderer willkommen geheißen. Aus den damals modernen Stilen vom Festland (besonders dem italienischen) und dem gälischen schuf Carolan eine einzigartige Mischform. Dennoch kann man nur Vermutungen darüber anstellen, in wieweit diese einheimische Tradition unter günstigeren Umständen die moderne Fiddle und die neuen Tanzrhythmen eingegliedert hätte. Obwohl das Harfen-Festival in Belfast im Jahre 1798 nur 10 Harfenisten anzog, wurden zumindest einige ihrer instrumentalen Weisen aufgeschrieben und erhielten sich so. Musiker des 20. Jahrhunderts, wie z.B. Derek Bell von *The Chieftains*, haben dieses Repertoire wieder in Umlauf gebracht.

In Gegenden wie Connemara oder Sliabh Luachra, in denen irisch gesprochen wird, überlebte auch eine Tradition des unbegleiteten Singens, das *sean-nós* (alter Stil), bei dem die Lieder mit rhythmischen und metrischen Mustern der gälischen Sprache und Dichtung durchsetzt sind. Parallel dazu gibt es eine englischsprachige Liedtradition in Irland. Die Melodien bzw. Weisen dieser Lieder können auch als Instrumentalsoli gespielt werden. Deren beste Interpreten sind wiederum jene, die ihre Texte kennen.

Die Struktur des Tanzliedes

In einem irischen Fiddlerepertoire bilden die Tanzlieder das Herzstück. In jedem achttaktigen Abschnitt des Liedes, die als Teil A und Teil B bezeichnet werden, ist die Musik in Phrasen von je zwei Takten untergliedert, den sich wiederholenden melodischen Bausteinen des Stückes. Man beginnt damit, die erste Phrase über das Hören zu lernen, und erst wenn man sie auswendig kann, fügt man die zweite hinzu. Die dritte und vierte Phrase innerhalb einer Abfolge wird man schneller beherrschen, da diese normalerweise das Eröffnungsmaterial, mit einem abgewandelten Ende, wiederholen. Danach spielt man den kompletten A-Teil mehrere Male auswendig durch, bevor man die gleiche Vorgehensweise auf das Erlernen des B-Teils anwendet.

Die Ästhetik irischer Tanzmusik basiert auf kreativer Wiederholung. Das Lied baut sich nicht langsam zu einem großartigen Höhepunkt hin auf, wie bei einem romantischen Stück, sondern kehrt immer wieder zu seinem eigenen Anfang zurück, wie die Symbole auf einer sich drehenden Gebetsmühle. Die Ich-Angst des Spielers, sogar der Drang nach Selbstdarstellung des Künstlers, lässt nach. Bewusster Gebrauch von Dynamik ist selten. Viel wichtiger ist bei jeder Tanzmusik der Gegensatz zwischen betonten und unbetonten Noten – egal, ob sie tatsächlich zum Tanzen gespielt wird oder nicht.

Tanzlied-Typen

Anmerkung: Die Tempoangaben beziehen sich hier darauf, wenn zum Tanz aufgespielt wird. Viele Musiker spielen langsamer. Ein gleichbleibender Puls und eine korrekte Verteilung der Akzente sind grundsätzlich wichtiger als metronomische ‚Genauigkeit'.

Der **Reel** wird flott im Alla-Breve-Takt gespielt, mit zwei halben Schlägen pro Takt (𝅗𝅥 = ca. 112/120). Feine

[1] *Aus Platzgründen werden die Stücke nur ein- oder zweimal hintereinander auf der CD gespielt*

Akzentverschiebungen zwischen der betonten und der unbetonten Zeit können von erfahreneren Spielern ausprobiert werden. Reels mit insgesamt nur 16 Takten statt der üblichen 32 werden *single reels* genannt.

Von den Jigs gibt es drei Arten: der *double jig* (♩. = ca. 126) steht im 6/8–Takt; der *slip-jig* (♩. = ca. 144) im 9/8–Takt; und der *single jig* oder *slide*, der besonders mit den Grafschaften Cork und Kerry assoziiert wird, steht im 12/8-Takt (♩.= 132-138). Der charakteristische ‚rhythmische Schwung' eines double jig mit seinen zwei Schlägen pro Takt wird dadurch erreicht, dass die erste Achtelnote auf Kosten der zweiten verlängert wird:

Beispiel 1

Hornpipes stehen auch im Alla-Breve-Takt, obwohl sie langsamer als Reels sind (𝅗𝅥 = ca. 92). Sie werden nicht wie notiert, sondern triolisch gespielt, d.h. die erste von jedem Achtelnotenpaar wird immer doppelt so lange gespielt wie die zweite:

Beispiel 2

Die gesamteuropäische Polka des 19. Jahrhunderts wird in Cork und Kerry normalerweise schnell (♩= ca. 132 –138) und im 2/4–Takt gespielt, oft auch mit einer betonten zweiten Zeit.

Der **German** (die Kurzform von ‚German schottische' [Deutsch- Schottischer], eine Art *Scheunentanz* und hauptsächlich mit der Grafschaft Donegal verbunden, wird im Alla-Breve-Takt (𝅗𝅥 = ca. 106) gespielt. Man kann ihn entweder so spielen wie notiert, oder triolisch wie eine Hornpipe.

Die Benutzung des Bogens

Außer im Fall von langsamen Airs neigen irische Spieler dazu, nicht mehr als ein Fünftel der Bogenlänge zu nutzen. Oft ist es sogar sehr viel weniger. Die Strichstelle befindet sich dabei gewöhnlich ungefähr im oberen zweiten Drittel des Bogens. Ein Wechsel zwischen aufeinanderfolgenden Momenten von Leichtigkeit und Schwere sind das Herz einer guten Tanzstil–Bogentechnik. Der Spieler muss immer die Zeit spüren, und das Klopfen mit dem Fuß ist nicht unüblich. Bindungen sind in dieser Ausgabe eingezeichnet, wobei die freiwilligen Bindungen (gepunktet eingetragen) für die ehrgeizigeren Spieler sind. Neueinsteiger werden das wahrscheinlich hilfreich finden. Erfahrenen Fiddlern im irischen Stil steht es selbstverständlich frei, sowohl die Bogen- als auch die Verzierungstechnik nach eigenem Gutdünken anzuwenden. Der Bogen bleibt meistens auf den Saiten und eine Vielzahl von Bogenmuster lassen den Rhythmus, je nach Liedtyp, klar erkennen. Viele Spieler verwenden gerne einen Abstrich für die allerletzte Note eines Liedes. Man sollte sich immer vor Augen halten, dass die Notation nur die horizontale *Richtung* des Bogens beschreibt, nicht aber ihr ‚vertikales' Ausmaß, das man fühlen muss.

Ganz allgemein gibt es zwei verschiedene Arten von Akzenten. Die von mir als *hart* bezeichneten Akzente werden durch die Attacke beim Beginn eines neuen Bogenstrichs (entweder auf oder ab) erzeugt und den meisten Violinisten vertraut sein. Statt den Bogen allerdings bewusst ‚herunterzudrücken', sollte man einfach nur das Gewicht seines Armes im Handgelenk und der Hand spüren. Unterarm und Handgelenk sollten sich wie ein Tänzer anfühlen, der sich in einem fortwährenden Spiel mit der Schwerkraft befindet. *Weiche* Akzente entstehen durch eine Zunahme der Bogengeschwindigkeit und des Armgewichts *mitten im Strich*, wobei man sich in die zweite von zwei gebundenen, oder die mittlere von drei Noten hineinlehnt. Man beginne den Bogenstrich leicht und übertrage dann das Gewicht seines Armes auf die starke Note.

Jigs haben zum Beispiel zwei betonte Noten in jedem Takt, nämlich jeweils die erste jeder Triole. Das *eine-Note-pro-Bogen*-Muster erzeugt einen Wechsel von Auf- und Abstrichen (harte Akzente) auf der Zeit. Wenn dieses Muster von einer Viertelnote durchbrochen wird, kann die ‚Normalität' durch eine Bindung zum nächsten betonten Schlag, einem weichen Akzent, wiederhergestellt werden.

Beispiel 3: Tom Billy's Favourite

The Wandering Minstrel kann komplett mit diesem Grundmuster gestrichen werden. Man kann auch die freiwilligen (gepunkteten) Bindungen im C-Teil ausprobieren. Dadurch werden mehr weiche Akzente in ein Muster eingeführt, das nach vier Takten ausklingt.

Beispiel 4: Wandering Minstrel

Ein nützliches Strichmuster für **Reels** und **Hornpipes**, ebenfalls mit ihrem *zwei-pro-Takt*-Schlag, ist das, was ich die 3-3-2-Strichart nenne. Hierbei werden in einem typischen Takt mit acht Achtelnoten die ersten drei einzeln gestrichen, die nächsten drei gebunden und die letzten zwei wieder einzeln gestrichen:

Beispiel 5: Over the Moor to Maggie

Genau wie in den Jigs erzeugt diese Strichart einen Wechsel zwischen Auf- und Abstrichakzenten auf den Schlägen. Allerdings ist der erste Akzent in diesem Fall hart, während der zweite, der auf die mittlere der drei gebundenen Noten fällt, weich ist.

Ein weiteres nützliches Muster für Reels ist die *ein-auf-drei-ab*-Strichart, die häufig zusammenmit einem ‚Cut' benutzt wird, um zwei Noten mit derselben Tonhöhe voneinander zu trennen:

Beispiel 6: Andy Davy´s, B1

Das nächste Beispiel, aus einer Hornpipe, benutzt drei weitere, allgemein übliche Streichtechniken: (i) eine Bindung über eine Triole hinaus; (ii) *Saitenwechsel* an Stellen, an denen die Bindungen über einen Schlag hinweggehen; und (iii) ein einzelner Abstrich zwischen zwei aufwärts gestrichenen Bindungen, was einen starken Akzent auf einer unbetonten Zeit erzeugt:

Beispiel 7: Home Brew

Polkas werden im Allgemeinen mit zwei Bogenstrichen pro Takt gespielt. Dabei empfindet man den (weichen) Akzent oft auf einer unbetonten Zeit, selbst bei einer punktierten Achtel, bei der das von der Notation her nicht ersichtlich ist:

Beispiel 8: Gullane Polka

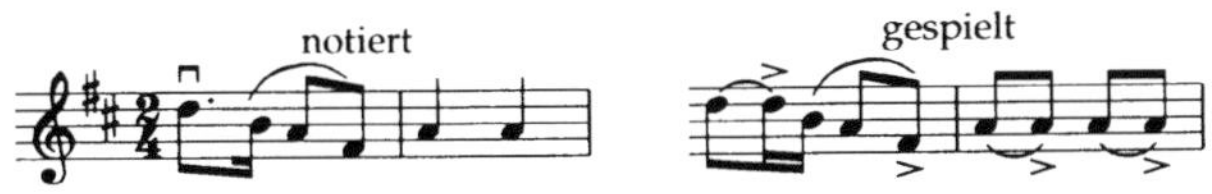

Manche Fiddler halten auch in Reels den Akzent auf der unbetonten Zeit für wichtiger als den auf der betonten. Auf jeden Fall besteht die Kunst darin, beim Zuhörer eine Erwartungshaltung zu erzeugen, um sie dann, vielleicht durch einen Wechsel der Strichart oder der Verzierungstechnik, kaum merkbar zu untergraben. Der *Roll* zum Beispiel führt eher zu einer Betonung der unbetonten Zeit.

Verzierungen
Auf welche Art man verziert, streicht oder die Melodie des jeweiligen Liedes abwandelt, ist Ausdruck der ganz persönlichen Kunst jedes Einzelnen. Die in diesem Buch verwendeten Zeichen für typische Verzierungsarten würden von einem erfahrenen traditionellen Spieler als überbezeichnet angesehen werden, und viele Verzierungen sind austauschbar. Flöten, [Tin-] Whistles, Uilleann-Dudelsäcke und andere Instrumente werden mit ähnlichen Verzierungen gespielt wie die Fiddle. Schwierige Verzierungen der Blasinstrumente werden zum Beispiel von den Fiddlern nachgespielt. Ganz allgemein haben die Verzierungen vor allem eine *rhythmische* Funktion.

Der **Roll** [Triller] besteht, genau wie der klassische Doppelschlag, aus fünf Tönen, die immer auf einem Bogenstrich aneinander gebunden sind und Wellenform besitzen: Hauptnote, eine Note höher, Hauptnote, eine Note tiefer und wieder die Hauptnote. Wenn die Hauptnote mit dem *ersten* Finger gespielt wird, wird die höhere Note üblicherweise mit dem *dritten*, nicht dem zweiten Finger gespielt.

Beispiel 9: Triller mit dem ersten, zweiten und dritten Finger

Genauso wie Rolls mit der Hauptnote auf dem ersten, zweiten oder dritten Finger, kann auch ein Triller mit leeren Saiten benutzt werden. Hier ein Beispiel aus einer Jig:

Beispiel 10: The Bank of Turf

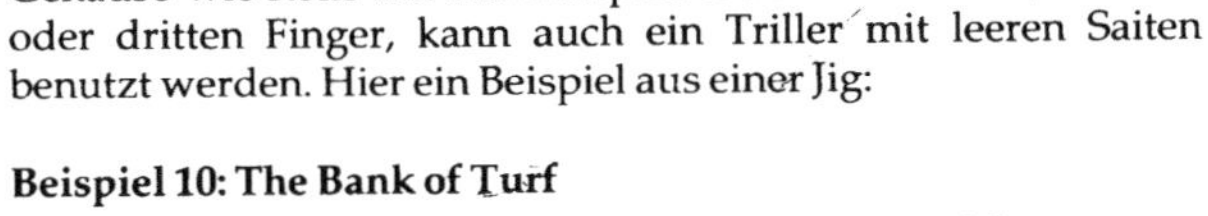

Anders als der Doppelschlag verlangt der Triller einen feinen aber dennoch starken Akzent mit dem Bogen auf der *unbetonten Zeit*, um einen schon beinahe perkussiven Effekt zu erzeugen. Der genaue Zeitpunkt des Akzentes innerhalb des fünfnotigen Clusters hängt ganz davon ab, ob die Hauptnote eine punktierte Viertel ist, die auf den Schlag fällt. In diesem Fall wird sie nämlich als **Long Roll** [langer Triller] gespielt:

Beispiel 11: Porthole of the Kelp

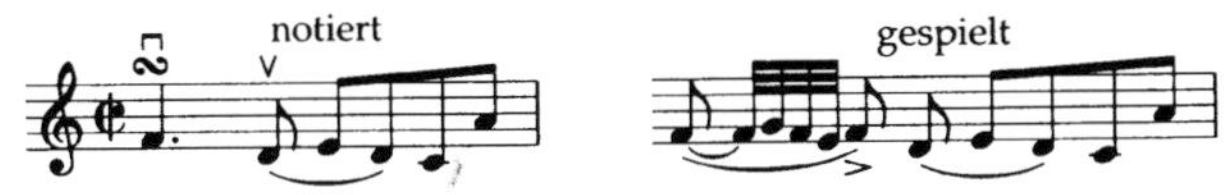

Oder der Triller wird über einer Viertel angezeigt, die sozusagen schon auf der unbetonten Zeit ist, obgleich ihr eine angebundene Achtel vorausgeht. In diesem Fall löst der Akzent mit dem Bogen den sogenannten **Short Roll** [kurzer Triller] aus:

Beispiel 12: Green Fields of Ros Beigh

Der **Slide** [Schleifer] ist ein *Portamento* der linken Hand, wobei die notierte Tonhöhe von einem Viertel- oder halben Ton tiefer ausgehend erreicht wird. Er wird gleichsam automatisch benutzt, um eine wichtige Note zu betonen.

Beispiel 13: Coach Road to Sligo

In dieser Sammlung wird der Slide nur über längeren Noten (durch einen Schrägstrich /) angezeigt.

Ein **Cut** [Schlag] ist ein leichter Schlag mit einem Finger auf die Saite. Er wird normalerweise verwendet, um eine Note zu betonen, und zwar oft in Verbindung mit der *ein-auf-drei-ab-*Strichart, um zwei gebundene Noten derselben Tonhöhe deutlicher zu artikulieren. Der dritte Finger wird üblicherweise verwendet, um eine mit dem ersten Finger gespielte Note zu verzieren.

Beispiel 14: Fergal O'Gara

Der perkussive, vom Bogen angetriebene **Treble** [Dreifacher], *shiver*, oder *shoogle* im schottischen Sprachgebrauch, hat bei der klassischen Violine keine Entsprechung. Die drei Noten werden nicht mit drei getrennten Strichen ‚gestrichen', wie es normal wäre, sondern durch das Zucken mit dem Handgelenk oder dem Arm wird ein schnelles Stottern des Bogens erzeugt. Es ist nicht ungewöhnlich, aus der letzten Note des Treble heraus (wie aus einer Triole, Beispiel 7) zu der nächsten Melodienote hin zu binden.

Beispiel 15: The Gravel Walks, B-Teil

In diesem Fall steht der Treble auf einer betonten Zeit. Genauso wie der Roll kann er aber auch benutzt werden, um einer unbetonten Zeit einen Akzent zu verleihen. Einige Spieler bevorzugen den Treble auf betonter, andere auf unbetonter Zeit. Dem letzteren gehen oft zwei Achtel voraus, die bei einem Abstrich gebunden werden:

Beispiel 16: The Flogging Reel

Der C-Teil von The Oak Tree verwendet abwechselnd Auf- und Abstrich-Trebles:

Beispiel 17: The Oak Tree

Ein ähnliches Zittern mit dem Bogen taucht in einigen Jigs auf:

Beispiel 18: Trip to Sligo

Manchmal werden sowohl Bordune auf leeren Saiten als auch Doppelgriffe benutzt.

Kirchentonarten und Vorzeichen

Die frühen Fiddler der ländlichen Gebiete benutzten als Grundlage für das Liedermachen ‚modale' Tonarten. In jener Zeit waren diese in der Kunstmusik zwar schon veraltet, aber vielleicht erlaubten sie ihnen, Elemente der älteren gälischen Musik zu übernehmen. Dieser Brauch wurde seitdem durchgängig weitergeführt.

Betrachten wir einmal die drei Reels aus der Gruppe 30. Alle stehen ‚in A', aber der erste, *Boys of Malin*, ist ionisch (= Dur) auf A, der dritte, *Dinkey's*, ist mixolydisch (große Terz, verminderte Septime), während *The Gravel Walks* dorisch ist (kleine Terz, große Sexte). Einer vierten Kirchentonart, dem Äolischen (kleine Terz, kleine Sexte), begegnet man in der irischen Musik ebenfalls (z.B. die *Fermoy Lasses*), aber nicht so häufig.

Die Vorzeichen stützen sich hier nicht auf das diatonische Dur/Moll-System, sondern folgen einer ‚volkstümlichen' Übereinkunft: Kreuze oder B's, die nicht tatsächlich im Lied vorkommen, werden nicht angegeben. Wenn also am Anfang eines Liedes zwei Kreuze angegeben sind, kann das D-ionisch, A-mixolydisch, E-dorisch oder, rein theoretisch, H-äolisch anzeigen. Es kommt ganz darauf an, welche Kirchentonart am besten zum Schlusston passt. Zum einfacheren Gebrauch ist hier die Kirchentonart eines jeden Liedes angegeben, obwohl man schnell den Bogen heraus hat, die ‚Tonika' oder den ‚Grundton' zu spüren, dem das Lied (normalerweise) zustrebt. Bei Liedern in den (ionischen) Durtonarten wird nur der Buchstabe angegeben. Irische Lieder auf E oder H haben fast ausnahmslos das ‚moll'-Klangbild der dorischen oder äolischen Kirchentonart. Einige Lieder, wie z.B. *Andy Davy's*, basieren auf einer pentatonischen Skala. Andere wiederum verbinden Kirchentonarten miteinander oder wechseln zwischen ihnen von einem Teil des Liedes zum anderen. Die dritte Stufe der Tonleiter kann auch mal völlig fehlen, wie in *Dan O, Keefe's Nr. 1* und *Tom Billy's Favourite*.

Viele ältere ländliche Spieler setzen bestimmte Töne der Tonleiter, besonders die Terz und die Sexte, als Vierteltöne zwischen dem leitereigenen und dem erhöhten Ton an. Solche ‚einsamen' Töne, die für jeden, der nur mit wohltemperierter Stimmung vertraut ist, ‚verstimmt' klingen mögen, sind mit einem Pfeil (↑ oder ↓) über dem Notensystem gekennzeichnet, und eine wertvolle Ausdrucksquelle.

Akkorde

Die alte Tradition der Soloaufführungen hat sich zu einer Ensemble-Tradition weiterentwickelt Diese spielen annäherungsweise ein eher ‚heterophones' Unisono, wobei alle Fiddlen, [Tin]-Whistles, Flöten, Concertinas, Uilleann-Dudel-säcke und Knopfakkordeons dieselbe Melodie spielen - *mehr oder weniger.* Die Frage, welche Akkorde man benutzen solle, hat sich erst gestellt, als Band-Arrangements entstanden, die das Klavier, die Gitarre und, seit den 60er Jahren des 20. Jahrhunderts, eine irische Version der griechischen Bouzouki miteinschlossen. Solange diese Frage noch nicht mal annäherungsweise mit Einstimmigkeit beantwortet worden ist, profitiert die traditionelle Musik von der Bereicherung an harmonischen Möglichkeiten aus der Kunstmusik des 20. Jahrhunderts. Die hier aufgeführten Akkorde, die als Buchstaben über dem Notensystem stehen, sind nur als Vorschläge zu verstehen. Am besten benutzt man sie als ‚offene' Akkorde, die weder die große noch die kleine Terz zu stark festlegen.

1

1

Slow Air

Lament for O'Donnell (G)

Fiddle player and teacher Pádraig O'Keeffe (1887–1963) from Gleanntán, East Kerry, was a highly influential musician in Sliabh Luachra, the Cork/ Kerry border region. He probably learned this lament, with its long, irregular phrases, from his grandmother's singing. Hugh Roe O'Donnell was an Irish chieftain whose defeat at the Battle of Kinsale in 1601 marked the beginning of the end of Gaelic Ireland.

1

Air lent

Lament for O'Donnell *(sol)*

Le violoniste et maître Padraig O'Keeffe (1887–1963) originaire de Gleanntán (East Kerry) fut un musicien très influent dans la région de Sliabh Luachra, aux confins de Cork et Kerry. Il apprit probablement de sa grand-mère ce chant de lamentation, avec ses longues phrases irrégulières. Hugh Roe O'Donnell était un chef irlandais dont la défaite à la bataille de Kinsale, en 1601, annonça la fin de l'Irlande gaélique.

1

Langsame Air

Lament For O'Donnell (G)

Der Fiddlespieler und Lehrer Pádraig O'Keeffe (1887–1963) aus Gleanntán in Ost Kerry, war ein Musiker, der auf Sliabh Luachra, die Grenzregion zwischen Cork und Kerry, großen Einfluss ausübte. Er lernte dieses Klagelied mit seinen langen, unregelmäßigen Phrasen durch den Gesang seiner Großmutter. Hugh Roe O'Donnell war ein irisches Clanoberhaupt, dessen Niederlage bei der Schlacht von Kinsale im Jahre 1601 den Beginn vom Ende des gälischen Irlands einläutete.

Lament for O'Donnell

2

2
Hornpipes
Julia Clifford's (A-dorian)
Sean Healy's (D)

Learned from Cork fiddle-player Seamus Creagh. Julia Clifford (1914–1997) and her brother Denis Murphy (1910–1974) were students of Padraig O'Keeffe. Sean Healy is a concertina player from West Cork. Remember that hornpipes are played with a triplet swing, and require free, fluid movements of the arm and wrist.

2
Hornpipes
Julia Clifford's (*la* dorien)
Sean Healy's (*ré*)

Ces deux pièces me furent transmises par Seamus Creagh, violoniste de Cork. Julia Clifford (1914–1997) et son frère Denis Murphy (1910–1974) étaient des disciples de Padraig O'Keeffe. Sean Healy est un joueur de concertina originaire du West Cork. Notez que les *hornpipes* sont mesurés selon une pulsation de triolets et réclament des mouvements libres et fluides du bras et du poignet.

2
Hornpipes
Julia Clifford's (A-dorisch)
Sean Healy's (D)

Julia Clifford (1914–1997) und ihr Bruder Denis Murphy (1910–1974) waren Studenten bei Pádraig O'Keeffe, nachdem sie bei dem Fiddlespieler Seamus Creagh aus Cork gelernt hatten. Sean Healy ist ein Concertina-Spieler und stammt aus West Cork. Man bedenke, dass Hornpipes triolisch gespielt werden und freie, flüssige Arm- und Handgelenksbewegungen erfordern.

Julia Clifford's

Sean Healy's

3

3

Double Jigs

Tom Billy's Favourite (A minor)
The Bank of Turf (D)

Tom Billy (1879–1944) was a blind fiddle player from Sliabh Luachra. Note the absence of either the minor or major third of A. Padraig O'Keeffe taught the second jig to Denis Murphy while cutting turf, marking out the notes with his spade. My own version is influenced by the playing of Donegal-born Paddy Glackin.

3

Double Jigs (double gigues)

Tom Billy's Favourite (*la* mineur)
The Bank of Turf (*ré*)

Tom Billy (1879–1944) était un violoniste aveugle de Sliabh Luachra. On observera l'absence de tierce, mineure ou majeure, du mode de *la*. Padraig O'Keeffe enseigna la deuxième gigue à Denis Murphy en traçant les notes avec sa pelle alors qu'il découpait des mottes de gazon *(turf)*. Ma propre version est influencée par l'interprétation de Paddy Glackin, natif de Donegal.

3

Double Jigs

Tom Billy's Favourite (a-Moll)
The Bank of Turf (D)

Tom Billy (1879–1944) war ein blinder Fiddlespieler aus Sliabh Luachra. Man beachte, dass es auf A weder eine große noch eine kleine Terz gibt. Pádraig O'Keeffe brachte Denis Murphy den zweiten Jig beim Torfstechen bei, wobei er die Noten mit seinem Spaten markierte. Meine eigene Version ist von der Spielweise des in Donegal geborenen Paddy Glackin beeinflusst.

Tom Billy's Favourite

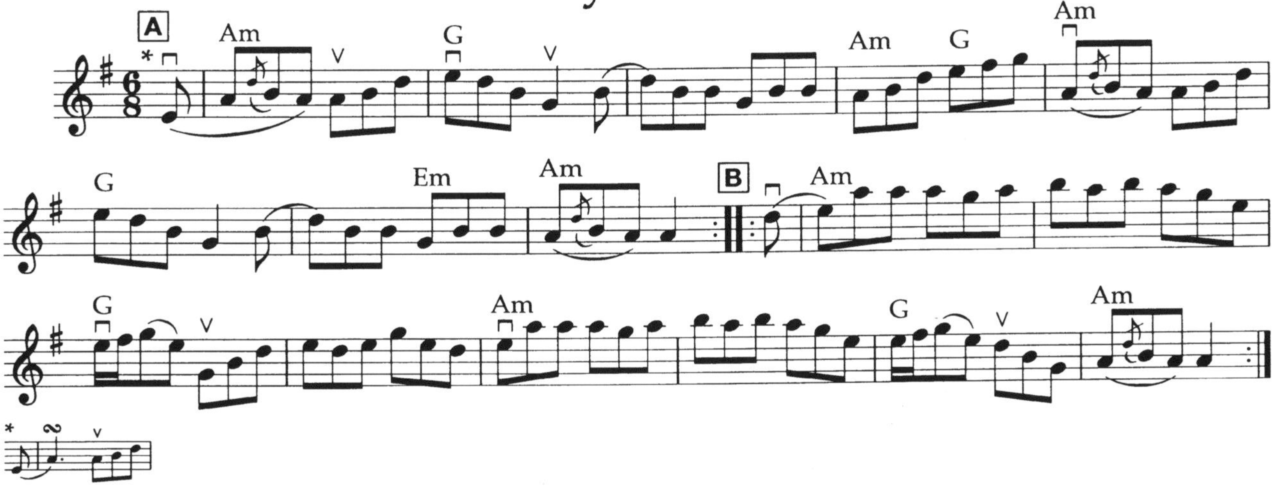

The Bank of Turf

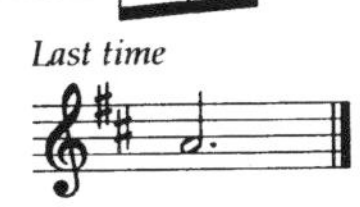

4

4
Slides
Scully Casey's (D-mixolydian)
Dan O'Keeffe's No. 1 (G)
Dan O'Keeffe's No. 2 (A minor)

Note the crotchet-quaver pattern of the slide rhythm. The first is from John 'Scully' Casey, father of famous Clare fiddler Bobby Casey (1926–2000). The others are from Sliabh Luachra, where quadrilles and other dances, probably first introduced by British army regiments in the 19th century, remain popular. In *O'Keeffe's No. 1*, note the use of half-sharps and, in *No. 2*, the absence of the minor or major third.

4
Slides
Scully Casey's (*ré* mixolydien)
Dan O'Keeffe's No. 1 *(sol)*
Dan O'Keeffe's No. 2 (*la* mineur)

Observez la formule en noires et croches du rythme de *slide*. Le premier est de John 'Scully' Casey, père du célèbre violoniste originaire de Clare, Bobby Casey (1926–2000). Les autres proviennent de Sliabh Luachra, où les quadrilles et autres danses, probablement amenés par les régiments de l'armée britannique au XIXe siècle, jouissent encore d'une grande popularité. Dans *O'Keeffe's No 1*, on notera l'utilisation de demi-dièses (quarts de ton) et, dans le No 2, l'absence de tierce mineure ou majeure.

4
Slides
Scully Casey's (D-mixolydisch)
Dan O'Keeffe's Nr. 1 (G)
Dan O'Keeffe's Nr. 2 (a-Moll)

Man beachte das Viertel-Achtel Muster des Slide-Rhythmus'. Der erste stammt von John „Scully" Casey, Vater des berühmten Fiedlers Bobby Casey (1926–2000) aus der Grafschaft Clare. Die anderen stammen aus Sliabh Luachra, wo Quadrillen und andere Tänze, die wahrscheinlich zuerst durch britische Regimenter im 19. Jahrhundert eingeführt wurden, weiterhin beliebt blieben. Man beachte in *O'Keeffe's Nr. 1* den Gebrauch von Vierteltonkreuzen und, in *Nr. 2*, das Fehlen von großer und kleiner Terz.

Scully Casey's

Dan O'Keeffe's Slide No. 1

Dan O'Keeffe's Slide No. 2

5

5

Slide/Polka

Nell O'Sullivan's (D)
The Gullane Polka (D)

In this set (for a dance called the Lancers) learned from fiddler Matt Cranitch and his band Sliabh Notes, the transition from slide to polka requires a constant beat, its time-value changing from dotted-crotchet to crotchet. *The Gullane Polka* began life as an 18th-century Scottish strathspey, *Cameron's Got His Wife Again*. Remember to give emphasis to the off-beat.

5

Slide/Polka

Nell O'Sullivan's *(ré)*
The Gullane Polka *(ré)*

Dans cet ensemble (destiné a une danse appelée *The Lancers* [les Lanciers]) appris auprès du violoniste Matt Cranitch et de son orchestre «Sliabh Notes», le passage du *slide* à la polka suppose une pulsation constante dont la valeur passe de la noire pointée à la noire. La *Gullane Polka* était à l'origine un *«strathspey»* écossais du XVIIIe siècle, *Cameron's Got His Wife Again*. N'oubliez pas de mettre en valeur la syncope.

5

Slide/Polka

Nell O'Sullivan's (D)
The Gullane Polka (D)

In dieser Gruppe (für einen Tanz namens Lancers), die ich von dem Fiddler Matt Cranitch und seiner Band Sliabh Notes gelernt habe, erfordert der Übergang vom Slide zur Polka ein durchgängiges Tempo, wobei der Grundschlag von einer punktierten Viertel zu einer Viertel wechselt. Die *Gullane Polka* begann ihren Entwicklungsweg im 18. Jahrhundert als schottischer Strathspey mit dem Namen *Cameron's Got His Wife Again*. Man achte darauf, die unbetonte Zeit zu betonen.

Nell O'Sullivan's

The Gullane Polka

6

6
Polkas
Toormore Polka No. 1 (D)
Toormore Polka No. 2 (D/A)
Two rousing (and easy) polkas that can also follow on directly from *The Gullane Polka* if a longer polka set is required.

6
Polkas
Toormore Polka No 1 *(ré)*
Toormore Polka No 2 *(ré/la)*
Deux polkas enlevées (et faciles) qui peuvent également suivre directement la *Gullane Polka* pour former une série plus longue.

6
Polkas
Toormore Polka Nr. 1 (D)
Toormore Polka Nr. 2 (D/A)
Zwei anregende (und leichte) Polkas, die man auch direkt anschließend an die *Gullane Polka* spielen kann, wenn eine längere Polka-Gruppe enforderlich ist.

Toormore Polka No. 1

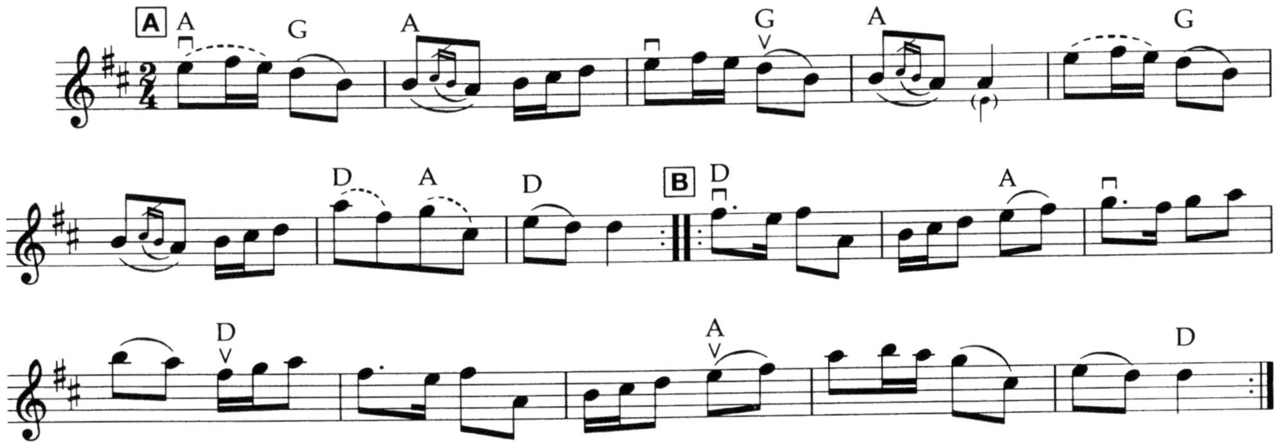

Toormore Polka No. 2

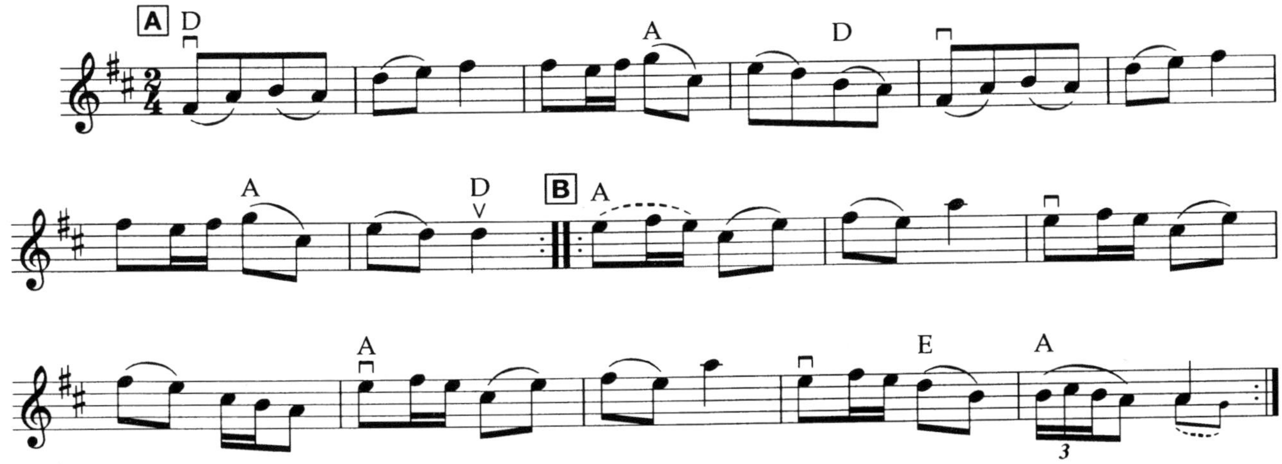

7

7
Polkas

Knocknaboul Polka (G)
Ballydesmond Polka No. 3 (D)

Named after local villages, polkas like these from Julia Clifford are deeply embedded in the Sliabh Luachra fiddle tradition. I try to capture some of the nuances of her ornamentation and bowing. Julia and her brother Denis recorded the second tune in a set with two other famous 'Ballydesmond' Polkas.

7
Polkas

Knocknaboul Polka *(sol)*
Ballydesmond Polka No 3 *(ré)*

Portant le nom de villages locaux, les polkas telles que celles-ci, dues à Julia Clifford, sont profondément enracinées dans la tradition du violon traditionnel *(fiddle)* de Sliabh Luachra. Je me suis efforcé de reproduire certaines des nuances de l'ornementation et des coups d'archet de Julia Clifford qui, en compagnie de son frère Denis, enregistra le deuxième air avec deux autres Polkas célèbres de Ballydesmond.

7
Polkas

Knocknaboul Polka (G)
Ballydesmond Polka Nr. 3 (D)

Polkas, wie die hier vorliegenden von Julia Clifford, sind tief in die Fiddletradition von Sliabh Luachra eingebettet und wurden nach dortigen Ortschaften benannt. Ich versuche, einige Feinheiten ihrer Verzierungs- und Streichkunst einzufangen. Julia und ihr Bruder Denis nahmen das zweite Lied in einer Gruppe mit zwei anderen berühmten Ballydesmond Polkas auf.

Knocknaboul Polka

Ballydesmond Polka No. 3

8

8

Reels

Fergal O'Gara (D)

Green Fields of Ros Beigh (E-dorian)

Two classic reels learned from London Irish fiddler Eilish Byrne. Fergal O'Gara was recorded by Michael Coleman (see Set 22). Ros Beigh is a coastal village in the Ring of Kerry. These are not the easiest of reels to play and you might prefer to start with, say, *Andy Davy's* or *Swinging on the Gate.*

8

Reels

Fergal O'Gara (*ré*)

Green Fields of Ros Beigh (*mi* dorien)

Ces deux *reels* classiques m'ont été transmis par le violoniste irlandais établi à Londres Eilish Byrne. *Fergal O'Gara* a été enregistré par Michael Coleman (voir pièces No 22). Ros Beigh est un village côtier situé le long du *Ring of Kerry* (route contournant le comté de Kerry). Ces deux pièces ne sont pas les *reels* les plus faciles à jouer et il sera peut-être préférable d'aborder cette forme avec *Andy Davy's* ou *Swinging on the Gate.*

8

Reels

Fergal O'Gara (D)

Green Fields of Ros Beigh (E-dorisch)

Zwei klassische Reels, die ich von dem in London lebenden irischen Fiddler Eilish Byrne gelernt habe. *Fergal O'Gara* wurde von Michael Coleman aufgenommen (s. Gruppe 22). Ros Beigh ist ein an der Küste gelegener Ort im Ring of Kerry. Diese hier sind zum Spielen nicht gerade die leichtesten Reels und der ein oder andere wird es vielleicht vorziehen, mit, sagen wir mal, *Andy Davy's* oder *Swinging on the Gate* anzufangen.

Fergal O'Gara

Green Fields of Ros Beigh

9

9

Clare Jigs

The Humours of Ennistymon (G)
The Kilfenora Jig (G)
The Cliffs of Moher (A-dorian)

Three classic Jigs from the West Clare tradition. Ennistymon is an attractive town with a 'salmon ladder', to allow the fish to swim upstream. The next two jigs, popular in sessions, also celebrate interesting and much-visited places in County Clare. The *Kilfenora* is sometimes called the *Clare Jig*, or the *Old Favourite*.

9

Clare Jigs

The Humours of Ennistymon *(sol)*
The Kilfenora Jig *(sol)*
The Cliffs of Moher (*la* dorien)

Ces trois gigues classiques appartiennent à la tradition de la région de Clare. Ennistymon est une jolie ville, fière de son «échelle des saumons» qui permet aux poissons de nager en remontant le courant. Les deux autres gigues, en faveur auprès du public, célèbrent des endroits intéressants et très visités du comté de Clare. La gigue *Kilfenora* est parfois connue sous le nom de *Clare Jig* ou *Old Favourite*.

9

Clare Jigs

The Humours of Ennistymon (G)
The Kilfenora Jig (G)
The Cliffs of Moher (A-dorisch)

Drei klassiche Jigs aus der Tradition des westlichen Clare. Ennistymon ist eine attraktive Stadt mit einer „Lachsleiter" damit die Fische stromaufwärts schwimmen können. Die nächsten beiden Jigs, die in Sessions sehr beliebt sind, preisen ebenfalls interessante und viel besuchte Plätze in der Grafschaft Clare. Der *Kilfenora* wird manchmal auch *Clare Jig* oder *Old Favourite* genannt.

The Humours of Ennistymon

The Kilfenora Jig

The Cliffs of Moher

10

10

Slow Air

Lament for Owen Roe O'Neill

(E-aeolian)

Irish hopes of their leader Owen Roe O'Neill were dashed when he was poisoned in 1649. This lamentation (in Irish, *Caoineadh Eoghain Rua)* was published in Petrie's *Ancient Music of Ireland*, though my phrasing here is based on the fiddle playing of Matt Cranitch, who first recorded it in 1969 with his band *Na Filí*. Nollaig Casey has also recorded a great version.

10

Air lent

Lament for Owen Roe O'Neill

(*mi* éolien)

Les espoirs fondés par les Irlandais sur leur chef Owen Roe O'Neill furent anéantis quand celui-ci fut empoisonné en 1649. Cette lamentation (en irlandais: *Caoineadh Eoghain Rua)* fut publiée dans le recueil *Ancient Music of Ireland* de Petrie. Mon phrasé ici se rattache au jeu du violoniste Matt Cranitch qui le premier l'a enregistrée avec son ensemble *Na Fili* en 1969. Nollaig Casey en a aussi enregistré une très belle version.

10

Langsame Air

Lament for Owen Roe O'Neill

(E-äolisch)

Die irischen Hoffnungen auf ihren Anführer Owen Roe O'Neill zerschlugen sich, als er im Jahre 1649 vergiftet wurde. Diese Wehklage (auf irisch heißt sie *Caoineadh Eoghain Rua)* wurde in Petrie's *Ancient Music of Ireland* veröffentlicht. Meine Phrasierungsart beruht hier jedoch auf dem Fiddlespiel von Matt Cranitch, der sie erstmals im Jahre 1969 mit seiner Band *Na Filí* aufnahm. Nollaig Casey hat ebenfalls eine bedeutende Version davon aufgenommen.

Lament for Owen Roe O'Neill

11

Reels

The Porthole of the Kelp (D-dorian)
Farewell to Miltown (G-mixolydian)

The first tune is by Bobby Casey (1926–2000), who mastered the music of his native West Clare, as well as much of East Clare and East Galway, before moving to London after the Second World war. The second, referring to Miltown Malbay, is by his early teacher Junior Crehan. Bare notation can scarcely do justice to the inventive spirit of Casey's playing.

11

Reels

The Porthole of the Kelp (*ré* dorien)
Farewell to Miltown (*sol* mixolydien)

Le premier air est de Bobby Casey (1926–2000), expert dans la musique de sa région natale du West Clare, de l'East Clare et de l'East Galway, installé à Londres après la seconde guerre mondiale. La deuxième pièce, référence à la ville de Miltown Malbay, est de son premier maître Junior Crehan. La simple notation ne peut complètement rendre sa juste mesure à l'esprit d'inventivité du jeu de Casey.

11

Reels

The Porthole of the Kelp (D-dorisch)
Farewell to Miltown (G-mixolydisch)

Das erste Lied ist von Bobby Casey (1926–2000), der sowohl die Musik seiner Heimat West Clare als auch die von Ost Clare und Ost Galway beherrschte, bevor er nach dem Zweiten Weltkrieg nach London übersiedelte. Das zweite Lied, das sich auf Miltown Malbay bezieht, ist von seinem früheren Lehrer Junior Crehan. Reine Notation kann dem erfinderischen Geist von Casey's Spiel kaum gerecht werden.

The Porthole of the Kelp

Bobby Casey

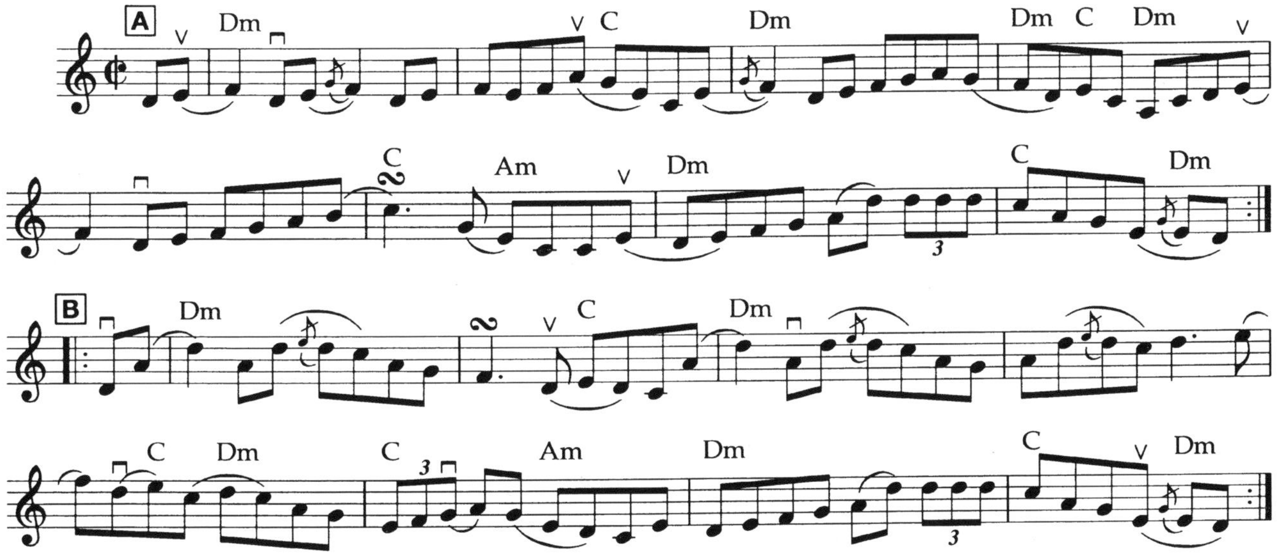

Farewell to Miltown

Junior Crehan

12

12

Hornpipes

The Plains of Boyle (D)
McGivney's Hornpipe (E-dorian)

The first is a well-known hornpipe with an attractive C-natural. The second, from Eamonn McGivney of Miltown Malbay, is a lovely 'setting', or version, of the *Cuckoo's Nest*, a tune also much played in England. I learned it from London-based flute-player Kathy Walton and whistle-player Sue Lee.

12

Hornpipes

The Plains of Boyle (*ré*)
McGivney's Hornpipe (*mi* dorien)

La première pièce est un *hornpipe* connu comportant un étonnant *do* naturel. La deuxième, due à Eamonn McGivney de Miltown Malbay, est une charmante version de *The Cuckoo's Nest*, air également beaucoup joué en Angleterre. Je l'ai appris auprès de Kathy Walton, flûtiste installée à Londres, et de Sue Lee, joueuse de sifflet.

12

Hornpipes

The Plains of Boyle (D)
McGivney's Hornpipe (E-dorisch)

Die erste ist eine bekannte Hornpipe mit einem reizvollen C. Die zweite, von Eamonn McGivney aus Miltown Malbay, ist eine hübsche „Vertonung", oder Version, von *Cuckoo's Nest*, einem Lied, das auch in England sehr häufig gespielt wird. Ich lernte sie von der Flötistin Kathy Walton, die hauptsächlich in London lebt, und der [Tin]-Whistle-Spielerin Sue Lee.

The Plains of Boyle

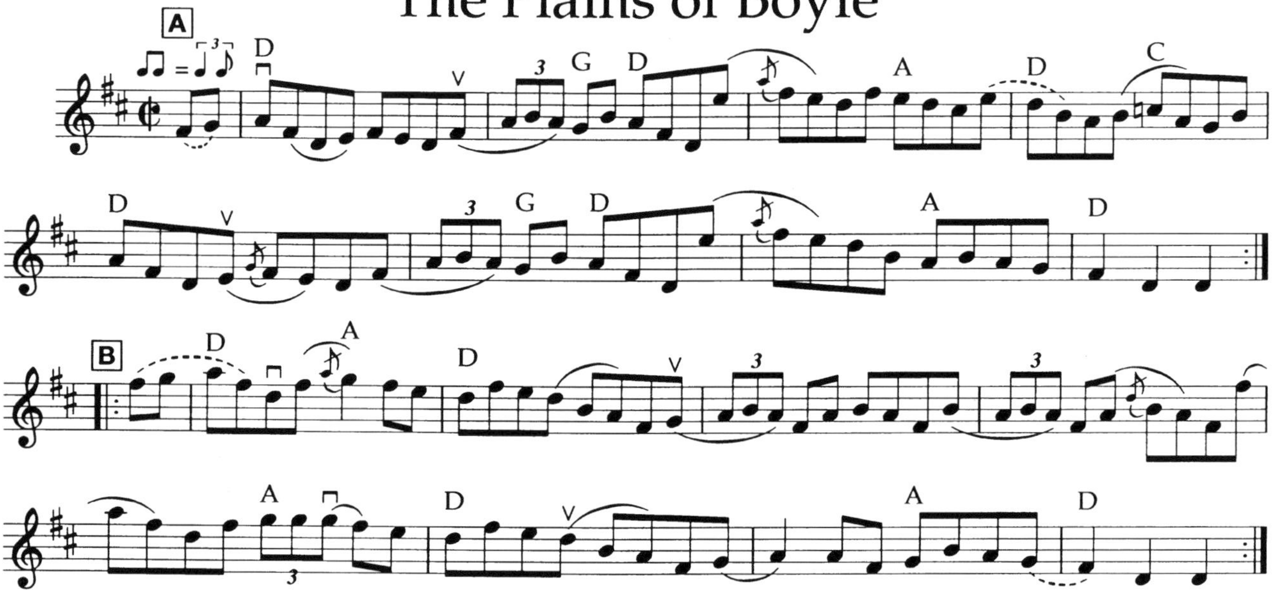

McGivney's Hornpipe

13

13
Polkas
Ballyhoura Mountains (G)
Lucy Farr's Polka (D minor)

Although polkas are usually associated with the south-west of Ireland, I learned these from the playing of East Galway fiddler, Lucy Farr (1912–2002). The pitch of the third degree of the scale in the second tune is ambiguous, The Fs in the A-part (which Lucy called 'lonesome notes') being played a quarter-tone sharp.

13
Polkas
Ballyhoura Mountains *(sol)*
Lucy Farr's Polka (*ré* mineur)

Quoique les polkas soient habituellement associées au sud-ouest de l'Irlande, celle-ci m'a été révélée en écoutant la violoniste de l'East Galway, Lucy Farr (1912–2002). La hauteur du troisième degré de l'échelle du deuxième air est ambiguë, les *fa* dans la partie en *la* (que Lucy appelait «notes solitaires») étant élevés d'un quart de ton.

13
Polkas
Ballyhoura Mountains (G)
Lucy Farr's Polka (d-Moll)

Obwohl man Polkas normalerweise mit dem Südwestern Irlands verbindet, lernte ich diese von der Fiedlerin Lucy Farr (1912–2002) aus Ost Galway. Im zweiten Lied ist die Tonhöhe der dritten Tonleiterstufe unklar. Im A-Teil werden die Fs (die Lucy die „einsamen Noten" nennt) mit einem Vierteltonkreuz gespielt.

Ballyhoura Mountains

Lucy Farr's Polka

14

14

Two Galway Reels

Andy Davy's (G)

The Pullet and the Cock (E minor)

The first of these two single reels from Lucy Farr uses a simple pentatonic scale. Andy Davy is, I believe, a Sligo fiddler. In bar B2 of the second tune the note C, the sixth degree of the scale, is played a quarter-tone sharp, another mode-bending 'lonesome note'.

14

Deux Reels de Galway

Andy Davy's *(sol)*

The Pullet and the Cock (*mi* mineur)

Le premier de ces deux *reels* indépendants de Lucy Farr est construit sur une gamme pentatonique simple. Andy Davy est, je crois, un violoniste de Sligo. Dans la mesure B2 du deuxième air, la note *do*, sixième degré l'échelle et autre «note solitaire» hors du mode, est élevée d'un quart de ton.

14

Zwei Galway Reels

Andy Davy's (G)

The Pullet and the Cock (e-Moll)

Lucy Farr benutzt für den ersten der beiden Single Reels eine einfache pentatonische Tonleiter. Soviel ich weiß, ist Andy Davy ein Fiddler aus Sligo. Im Takt B2 des zweiten Liedes wird die Note C, die sechste Tonleiterstufe, um einem Viertelton erhöht – eine weitere „einsame Note" die die zugrunde liegende Tonart verbiegt.

Andy Davy's

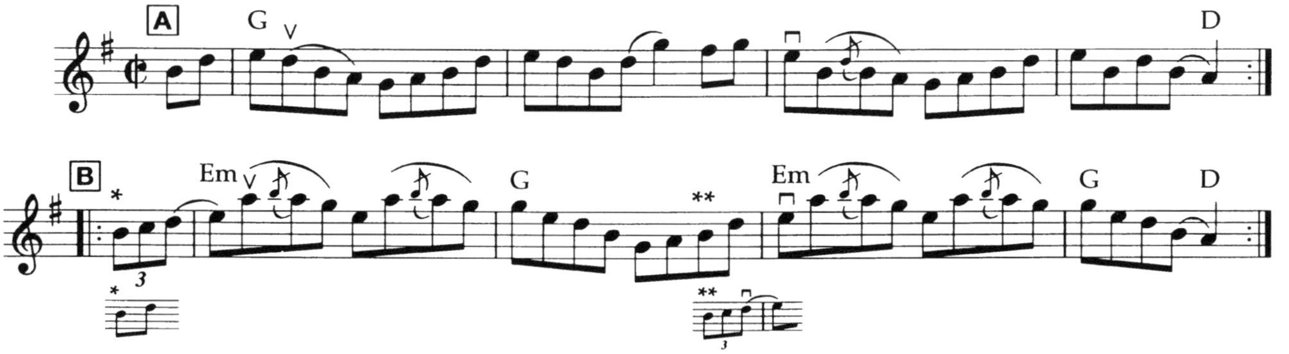

The Pullet and the Cock

15

15

Single Jigs

Music on the Wind (D)
The Lonesome Jig (D)

Slides are often played for set-dancing, but these two are 'listening tunes'. The first was composed by Lucy Farr around 1972. The second is also known as *The Rolling Wave*. Lucy was a very down-to-earth person. Once, noticing that she was playing with her bow over the fingerboard, I asked her if this was a 'traditional' bowing technique. 'Ah no,' said Lucy, adjusting her glasses, 'it's just these bi-focals. I can't see properly'.

15

Simple Jigs (gigues simples)

Music on the Wind *(ré)*
The Lonesome Jig *(ré)*

Contrairement aux *slides* habituellement destinés à la danse en figures de groupe, ceux-ci sont des «airs à écouter». La premier fut composé par Lucy Farr vers 1972. Le second est également connu comme *The Rolling Wave*. Lucy était quelqu'un de très pratique. Un jour, ayant remarqué qu'elle jouait avec l'archet au-dessus de la touche, je lui demandai s'il s'agissait d'une technique de coup d'archet «traditionelle». «Ah non!» répondit-elle en remontant ses lunettes «c'est à cause de ces doubles foyers. Je ne vois pas bien.»

15

Single Jigs

Music on the Wind (D)
The Lonesome Jig (D)

Beim Set-Dancing [einer irischen Art von Square-Dance. Anm. d. Ü.] werden oft Slides gespielt, aber diese beiden sind „Lieder zum Zuhören". Das erste wurde um das Jahr 1972 von Lucy Farr komponiert. Das zweite ist auch unter dem Namen *The Rolling Wave* bekannt. Lucy war eine sehr nüchterne Person. Einmal bemerkte ich, dass bei ihrem Spiel der Bogen über dem Griffbrett war. Ich fragte sie, ob das eine „traditionelle" Strichtechnik sei. „Aber nein", sagte Lucy und rückte ihre Brille zurecht, „es ist nur diese Zweistärkenbrille. Ich kann einfach nicht richtig damit sehen".

Music on the Wind

Lucy Farr

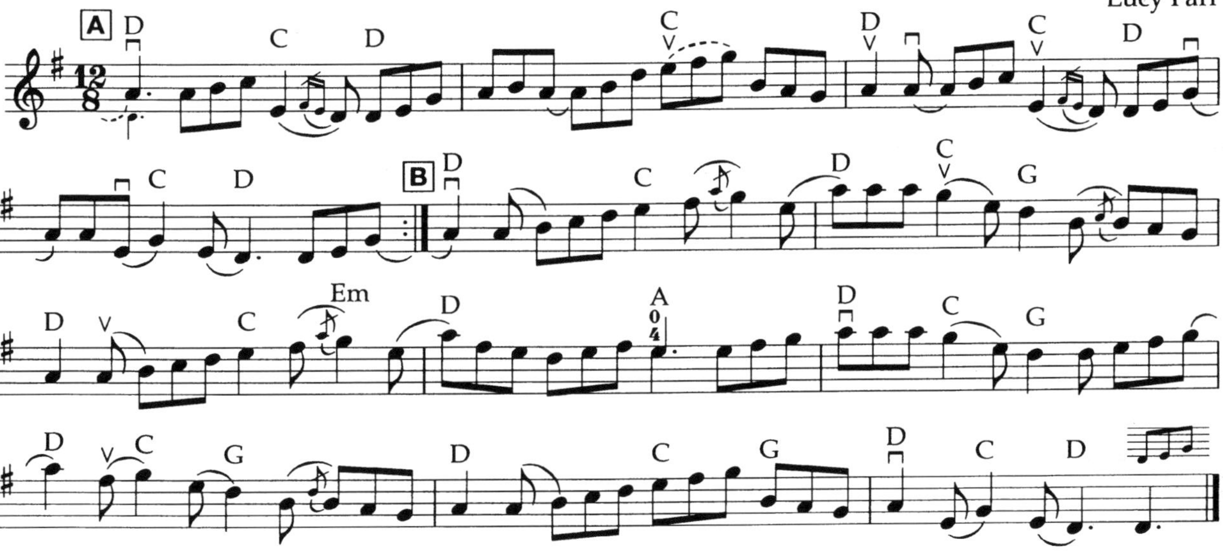

The Lonesome Jig

16

16

Two Hornpipes

The Home Brew (D-mixolydian)
Galway Bay Hornpipe (G minor)

Hornpipes, remember, are played with a triplet swing, i.e., with the first of each pair of quavers twice as long as the second, though this is not shown in the notation. The modal character of the first tune contrasts with the more classical-sounding G minor of the second, which I learned from the fiddle playing of Tommy Peoples.

16

Deux Hornpipes

The Home Brew (*ré* mixolydien)
Galway Bay Hornpipe (*sol* mineur)

On a vu que les *hornpipes* sont joués selon une pulsation ternaire, c'est-à-dire que la première croche d'une paire y est deux fois plus longue que la deuxième bien que cela n'apparaisse pas dans la notation. Le caractère modal du premier air contraste avec la qualité plus classique du *sol* mineur du deuxième que j'ai appris en écoutant jouer Tommy Peoples.

16

Zwei Hornpipes

The Home Brew (D-mixolydisch)
Galway Bay Hornpipe (g-Moll)

Man erinnere sich bitte daran, dass Hornpipes triolisch gespielt werden, wobei die erste Note von jedem Achtelpaar doppelt so lang ist wie die zweite, obwohl dies nicht in der Notation zu sehen ist. Der kirchentonartige Charakter des ersten Liedes steht in Gegensatz zu dem eher klassisch klingenden g-Moll des zweiten. Gelernt habe ich sie von dem Fiddlespieler Tommy Peoples.

The Home Brew

Galway Bay Hornpipe

17

17
Instrumental Air
Michael O'Connor (E-aeolian)

Turloch Carolan (1670–1738) grew up in County Roscommon. At the age of eighteen, blinded by smallpox, he learned to play the harp and became a respected itinerant musician, dedicating his many compositions to various hosts and patrons. I learned this piece from fiddle player Nollaig Casey, who calls it *Michael Ward*. Some grace notes are used to indicate the harp chords.

17
Air instrumental
Michael O'Connor (*mi* éolien)

Turloch Carolan (1670–1738) grandit dans le comté de Roscommon. A l'âge de dix-huit ans, devenu aveugle après avoir contracté la variole, il étudia la harpe et devint un musicien itinérant respecté qui dédia ses nombreuses compositions à divers hôtes ou mécènes. Cette pièce, qu'elle intitule *Michael Ward*, m'a été transmise par la violoniste Nollaig Casey. Quelques notes d'agrément indiquent les emplacements des accords de harpe.

17
Instrumentale Air
Michael O'Connor (E-aölisch)

Turloch Carolan (1670–1738) wuchs in der Grafschaft Roscommon auf. Als Folge einer Pockenerkrankung erblindete er, erlente aber mit 18 Jahren das Harfenspiel und wurde ein angesehener, umherziehender Musiker, der seine vielen Kompositionen den unterschiedlichen Gastgebern und Gönnern widmete. Ich lernte dieses Stück von der Fiddlerin Nollaig Casey, die es *Michael Ward* nennt. Einige Verzierungen werden benutzt, um die Harfenakkorde anzudeuten.

Michael O'Connor

18

18

Instrumental Air

The Princess Royal (A-aeolian)

Carolan composed this air for a daughter of the 'Prince of Coolavin', as the head of the MacDermot family was known. Later used in a small opera, *The Lock and Key* (1796), the tune gained poular currency in both Ireland and England, and was assimiliated into folk fiddle tradition. This version, in hornpipe rhythm, is from fiddler Liam Rowsome.

18

Air instrumental

The Princess Royal (*la* éolien)

Carolan composa cet air pour une fille du "Prince de Coolavin", surnom donné au chef de la famille MacDermott. Introduit plus tard dans un petit opéra *The Lock and Key* (1796), cet air acquis la popularité tant en Irlande qu'en Angleterre et s'intégra à la tradition du *fiddle*. Cette version, sur un rythme de *hornpipe*, est due au violoniste Liam Rowsome.

18

Instrumentale Air

The Princess Royal (A-äolisch)

Das Oberhaupt der Familie MacDermot war als „Prinz von Coolavin" bekannt' und Carolan komponierte diese Weise für eine seiner Töchter. Dieses Lied wurde sowohl in Irland als auch in England sehr populär und in die Volkstradition der Fiddlemusik aufgenommen. Später wurde es sogar in der kleinen Oper *The Lock and Key* (1796) benutzt. Die vorliegende Version, im Rhythmus einer Hornpipe, ist von dem Fiddler Liam Rowsome.

The Princess Royal

19

19

Instrumental Air

Fanny Power (G)

A Carolan composition in stately jig-time for Fanny (Frances) Power of Loughrea, who married Richard Trench in 1732. Donal O'Sullivan's scholarly edition of Carolan's music (1958) gives the tune in the key of F, but these days it's more commonly played, as here, in G.

19

Air instrumental

Fanny Power (*sol*)

Cette gigue majestueuse de Carolan est dédiée à Fanny (Frances) Power de Loughrea qui épousa Richard Trench en 1732. L'édition savante de la musique de Carolan, établie par Donal O'Sullivan en 1958, restitue l'air dans la tonalité de *fa*, mais il est plus communément joué de nos jours en *sol*, comme ici.

19

Instrumentale Air

Fanny Power (G)

Eine in einem würdevollen Jig-Takt geschriebene Komposition von Carolan für Fanny (Frances) Power of Loughrea, die im Jahre 1732 Richard Trench heiratete. Donal O'Sullivan's gelehrte Ausgabe von Carolan's Musik (1958) gibt F als Tonart des Liedes an, aber heutzutage wird sie üblicherweise, wie hier auch, in G gespielt.

Fanny Power

20

20

Slip Jigs

The Dusty Miller (D)

A Fig for a Kiss (E-dorian)

The Dusty Miller has also been played by English fiddlers since the eighteenth century, but as a 3/2 hornpipe. As a slip jig it was recorded by Eilish O'Connor of Dundalk. The second tune was recently recorded by *The London Lasses*, who learned it from flute-player Kathy Walton.

20

Slip Jigs

The Dusty Miller (*ré*)

A Fig for a Kiss (*mi* dorien)

Dusty Miller figure également au répertoire des violonistes traditionnels anglais depuis le XVIIIe siècle mais sous forme de *hornpipe* à 3/2. La pièce a été enregistrée par Eilish O'Connor de Dundalk comme *slip-jig*. Le deuxième air, recueilli auprès de la flûtiste Kathy Walton, a été récemment enregistré par l'ensemble London Lasses.

20

Slip Jigs

The Dusty Miller (D)

A Fig for a Kiss (E-dorisch)

Set dem 18. Jahrhundert wurde *The Dusty Miller* auch von englischen Fiddlern gespielt, aber als Hornpipe im 3/2-Takt. Als Slip Jig wurde sie von Eilish O'Connor aus Dundalk aufgenommen. Das zweite Lied wurde kürzlich von *The London Lasses* aufgenommen, die es wiederum von der Flötistin Kathy Walton gelernt haben.

The Dusty Miller

A Fig for a Kiss

21

21
Slip Jig/Double Jigs
O'Farrell's Welcome to Limerick (D)
The Wandering Minstrel (D)
Donnybrook Fair (G)

Different tune-types are rarely played in the same set. The slip-jig/double jig combination is an exception. Piper Patrick O'Farrell, who performed on the London stage in 1791, composed the the first tune, whose Irish name, *An Phis Fliuch,* describes the rousing effect of his piping on some female listeners. The annual fair at Donnybrook, now in Dublin, was banned in 1855 because of disorderly behaviour.

21
Slip Jig/Double Jigs
O'Farrell's Welcome to Limerick *(ré)*
The Wandering Minstrel *(ré)*
Donnybrook Fair *(sol)*

Il est rare que différentes formes d'airs soient regroupées dans le même ensemble. L'association *slip-jig/double jig* est donc exceptionnelle. Piper Patrick O'Farrell, qui se produisant sur les scènes londoniennes en 1791, a composé le premier air dont le titre irlandais, *An Phis Fliuch,* décrit l'excitation provoquée par son jeu sur certaines de ses auditrices. La foire annuelle de Donnybrook, localité maintenant rattachée à Dublin, fut interdite en 1855 à cause des troubles qu'elle entraînait.

21
Slip Jig/Double Jigs
O'Farrell's Welcome to Limerick (D)
The Wandering Minstrel (D)
Donnybrook Fair (G)

Nur sehr selten werden unterschiedliche Lied-Typen in ein derselben Gruppe gespielt. Die Kombination von Slip Jig und Double Jig ist daher eine Ausnahme. Der Pfeifer Patrick O'Farrell, der 1791 in London auftrat, komponierte das erste Lied, dessen irischer Titel *An Phis Flich* den anregenden Effekt beschreibt, den Farrells Pfeifen auf einige seiner weiblichen Zuhörer hatte. Der einmal im Jahr stattfindende Jahrmarkt in Donnybrook, heute in Dublin, wurde im Jahre 1885 wegen „liederlichem" Benehmen verboten.

O'Farrell's Welcome to Limerick

The Wandering Minstrel

* Omit anacrusis to link with previous piece.

* Ne pas jouer l'anacrouse si on enchaîne à la pièce précédente.

* Um das Stück mit dem vorangehenden zu verbinden, Auftakt weglassen.

Donnybrook Fair

22

22

Double Jigs

The Coach Road to Sligo (D)
The Trip to Sligo (E-aeolian)
Coleman's Cross (E-dorian/G)

South-west Sligo in the early 1900s was populated by fiddle (and flute) players of genius. Several emigrated to America, including James Morrison, Paddy Killoran and, most famously, Michael Coleman (1891–1946), whose birthplace in Killavil the third tune honours. His 78rpm records made him Irish fiddle music's first transatlantic star. The fluid and ornate Sligo fiddle style is rightly admired, and widely copied, sometimes badly.

22

Double Jigs

The Coach Road to Sligo (*ré*)
The Trip to Sligo (*mi* éolien)
Coleman's Cross (*mi* dorien/*sol*)

Dans les années 1900, la ville de Sligo, dans le sud-ouest de l'Irlande, était peuplée de violonistes et de flûtistes traditionnels de génie. Plusieurs d'entre eux émigrèrent aux Etats-Unis, parmi lesquels James Morrison, Paddy Killoran et, le plus célèbre, Michael Coleman (1891–1946) dont le troisième air célèbre la ville natale de Killavil. Ses enregistrements en 78 tours lui valurent d'être la première vedette du fiddle irlandais outre-atlantique. Le style violonistique de Sligo, souple et orné, est, à juste titre, très admiré et largement imité, quoique parfois imparfaitement.

22

Double Jigs

The Coach Road to Sligo (D)
The Trip to Sligo (E-äolisch)
Coleman's Cross (E-dorisch/G)

Im frühen 19. Jahrundert waren in Südwest Sligo geniale Fiddle- (und Flöten-) Spieler beheimatet. Einige wanderten nach Amerika aus, darunter James Morrison, Paddy Killoran und Michael Coleman (1891–1946), der berühmteste von ihnen. Das dritte Lied ehrt Coleman's Geburtsort in Killavil. Seine Aufnahmen mit 78 U/min. machten ihn zum ersten Star der irischen Fiddlemusik aus Übersee. Der flüssige und reich verzierte Fiddlestil aus Sligo wird zu Recht bewundert und oft nachgeahmt, wenn auch manchmal schlecht.

The Coach Road to Sligo

The Trip to Sligo

Coleman's Cross

23

23

Sligo Reels

Martin Wynne's No. 1 (D)
No. 2 (B-aeolian)
No. 3 (G)

Martin Wynne (1916–1998) composed these reels in his twenties. Born in Bunnanadan, near Ballymote, County Sligo, he moved to London, where he played in ceilidh bands, before emigrating in 1948 to New York. The first two reels are more widely known than the third, which comes from Brian Conway. Traditional players rarely slow down, or end a set with a chordal flourish; they just stop. However, the type of ending given here may be used instead.

23

Sligo Reels

Martin Wynne's No 1 *(ré)*
No 2 *(si* éolien)
No 3 *(sol)*

Martin Wynne (1916–1998), qui composa ces *reels* vers l'âge de vingt ans, est né à Bunnanadan, près de Ballymote, dans le comté de Sligo. Il s'installa à Londres, où il jouait dans des ensembles ceilidh, puis émigra à New-York en 1948. les deux premiers *reels* sont plus largement connus que le troisième, transmis par Brian Conway. A la fin d'une série, les musiciens traditionnels ne ralentissent ou n'arpègent un accord final qu'à de rares occasions. Ils s'arrêtent tout simplement. Toutefois, la formule de conclusion qui apparaît ici peut aussi terminer un morceau.

23

Sligo Reels

Martin Wynne's Nr. 1 (D)
Nr. 2 (H-äolisch)
Nr. 3 (G)

Martin Wynne (1916–1998) komponierte diese Reels, als er zwischen 20 und 30 Jahre alt war. Er wurde in der Grafschaft Sligo, und zwar in Bunnanadan, in der Nähe von Ballymote, geboren, zog dann aber nach London, wo er in Ceilidh Bands mitspielte, bevor er im Jahre 1948 nach New York auswanderte. Die ersten zwei Reels sind deutlich bekannter als der dritte, der von Brian Conway stammt. Traditionelle Spieler werden am Ende einer Gruppe selten langsamer oder enden mit einem akkordischen Feuerwerk; sie hören einfach auf. Dennoch kann man auch die hier gespielte Schlussform einmal benutzen.

Martin Wynne's Number 1

Martin Wynne's Number 2

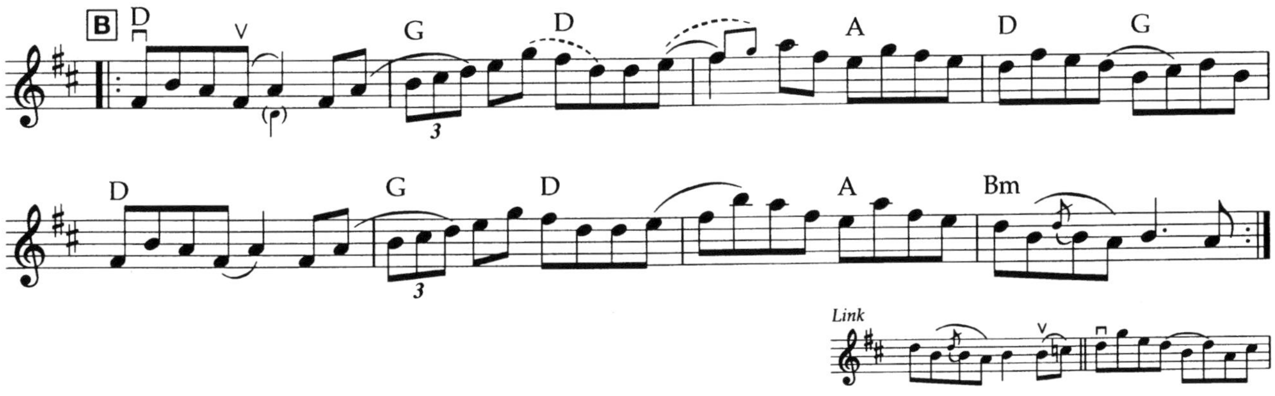

Martin Wynne's Number 3

24

24

Air

The Coulin (G)

Supposedly the ancient air, or melody, of a defiant and patriotic love song about a youth with long, flowing locks, a hairstyle banned in Ireland by the English colonial rulers. My version is influenced by that in the 1927 Roche collection, as well as by fiddler David Breen of Belfast.

24

Air

The Coulin *(sol)*

Il semble que cette mélodie ancienne fut celle d'une chanson d'amour rebelle et patriotique décrivant un jeune homme aux longues boucles libres, coiffure interdite en Irlande par les gouvernants coloniaux anglais. Ma version est marquée par celle reproduite dans le recueil Roche de 1927 et par celle du violoniste David Breen de Belfast.

24

Air

The Coulin (G)

Man nimmt an, dass dies die alte Air, oder Melodie, eines trotzigen und patriotischen Liebesliedes über einem jungen Mann mit langen, fließenden Locken ist. Dazu muss man wissen, dass diese Haartracht in Irland von den englischen Kolonialherrschern verboten wurde. Meine Version ist sowohl von derjenigen aus der *Roche*-Sammlung aus dem Jahre 1927, als auch von dem Fiedler David Breen aus Belfast beeinflusst.

The Coulin

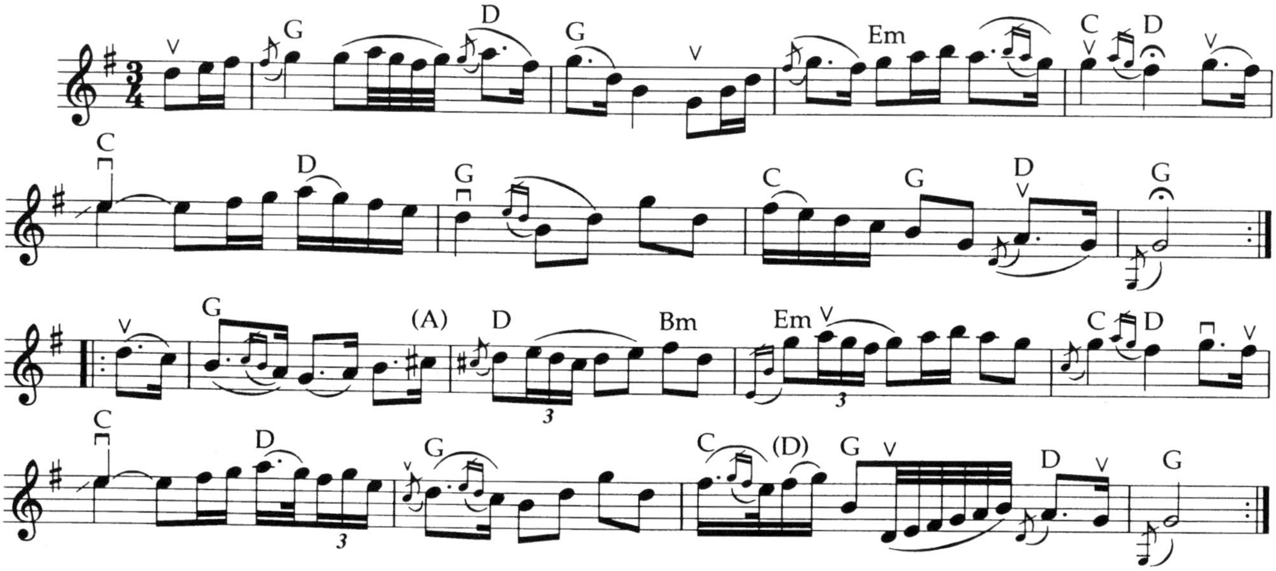

25

25

Reels in G

Swinging on the Gate (G)

Over the Moor to Maggie (G)

These two reels in G, a favourite key among flute players, were learned from Kathy Walton and Sue Lee. In North London pub sessions with fiddler Bridie Staunton they are often followed by *Craig's Pipes* (see No. 27), the three being known collectively as 'Bridie's Set'.

25

Reels en sol

Swinging on the Gate (sol)

Over the Moor to Maggie *(sol)*

Ces deux *reels* en *sol*, tonalité préférée des flûtistes, ont été recueillis auprès de Kathy Walton et de Sue Lee. Pendant les sessions qui ont lieu dans les pubs du nord de Londres avec le violoniste Bridie Staunton, ces pièces sont suivies de *Craig's Pipes* (voir No 27), l'ensemble des trois étant connu sous le nom de «Bridie's Set».

25

Reels in G

Swinging on the Gate (G)

Over the Moor to Maggie (G)

Diese beiden Reels in G, was nebenbei bei Flötisten eine Lieblingstonart ist, habe ich von Kathy Walton und Sue Lee gelernt. Wenn die Fiddlerin Bridie Staunton sie bei seinen Pub-Sessions in Nord-London spielt, lässt sie danach oft *Craig's Pipes* (s. Nr. 27) folgen. Alle drei zusammen sind auch als „Bridie's Set" bekannt.

Swinging on the Gate

Over the Moor to Maggie

26

26

A minor Reels

The Sligo Maid (A-dorian)

The Star of Munster (A-dorian)

A recording by Sligo-born dance fiddler Paddy Killoran (1904–1965) in 1930s New York helped to popularise the first reel. The second refers to the southernmost of Ireland's four ancient provinces. With two tunes so similiar in character, the one will often drive the other from your memory unless you consciously juxtapose them as a set.

26

Reels en la *mineur*

The Sligo Maid (*la* dorien)

The Star of Munster (*la* dorien)

Un enregistrement réalisé par le violoniste de danse natif de Sligo Paddy Killoran (1904–1965), à New York dans les années 1930, a popularisé le premier *reel*. Le second fait référence à la plus méridionale des quatre anciennes provinces irlandaises. Deux airs de caractère aussi semblable, peuvent se confondre dans la mémoire à moins de les juxtaposer.

26

Reels in a-Moll

The Sligo Maid (A-dorisch)

The Star of Munster (A-dorisch)

Der in Sligo geborenen Tanzfiddler Paddy Killoran (1904–1965) machte in den 30er-Jahren des 20. Jahrhunderts eine Aufnahme in New York, die dazu beitrug, den ersten Reel bekannt zu machen. Der zweite bezieht sich auf die am südlichsten gelegene der vier alten Provinzen Irlands. Bei zwei Liedern, die sich vom Charakter her so ähneln, wird man oft das eine über das Hören des zweiten vergessen, außer man stellt sie in einer Gruppe ganz bewusst nebeneinander.

The Sligo Maid

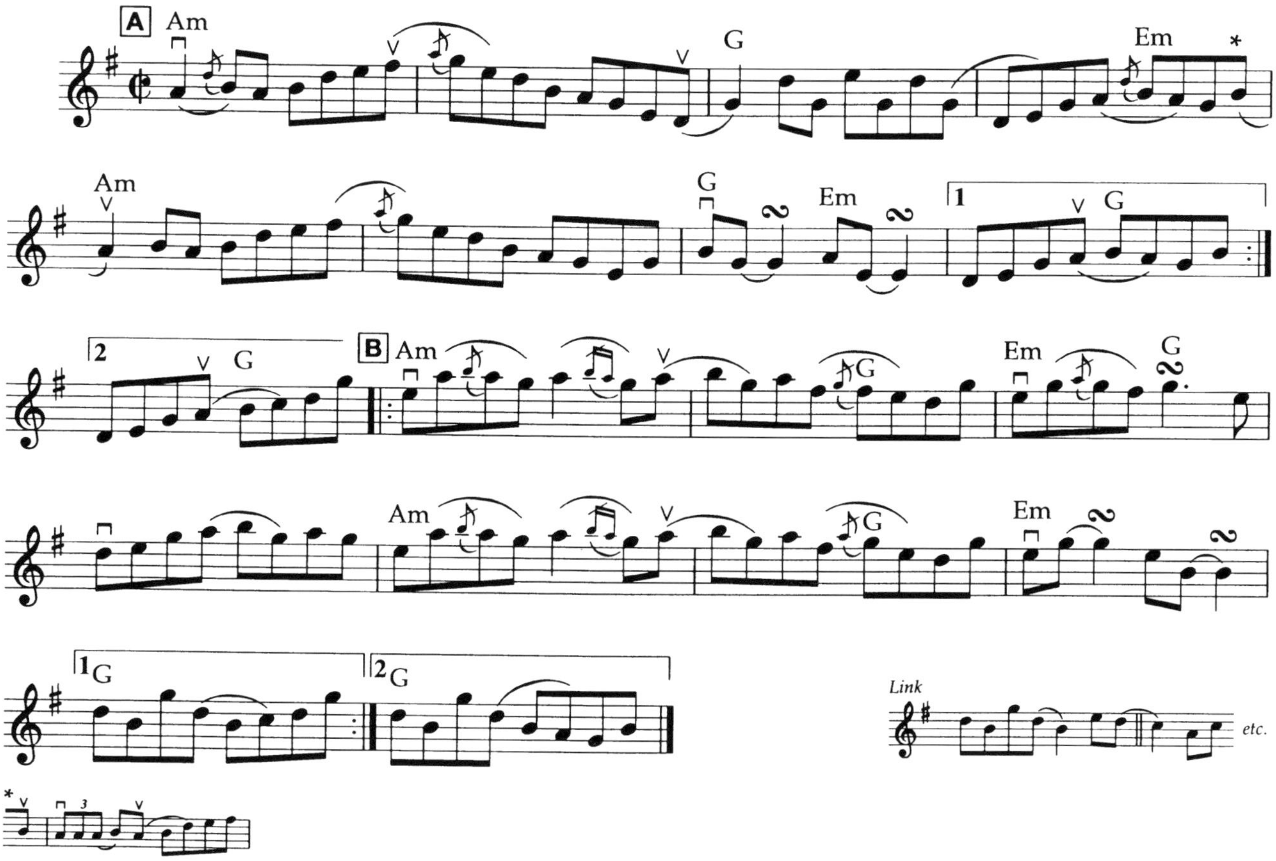

The Star of Munster

27

27
Reels
The Christmas Eve (G)
The Fermoy Lasses (E-aeolian)
Craig's Pipes (G)

The first reel was composed, I believe, by Irish-American musician Tommy Coen. The second is one of a relatively small number of Irish tunes in the Aeolian mode. I learned the third from Kathy Walton and Sue Lee.

27
Reels
The Christmas Eve *(sol)*
The Fermoy Lasses (*mi* éolien)
Craig's Pipes *(sol)*

Le premier *reel* fut composé, je crois, par le musicien irlando-américain Tommy Coen. Le deuxième appartient à un nombre relativement restreint d'airs irlandais en mode éolien. J'ai appris le troisième auprès de Kathy Walton et de Sue Lee.

27
Reels
The Christmas Eve (G)
The Fermoy Lasses (E-äolisch)
Craig's Pipes (G)

Der erste Reel wurde, glaube ich, von dem irisch-amerikanischen Musiker Tommy Coen komponiert. Der zweite ist eines von einer relativ kleinen Anzahl irischer Lieder, die in äolisch stehen. Den dritten lernte ich von Kathy Walton und Sue Lee.

The Christmas Eve

The Fermoy Lasses

Craig's Pipes

28

28

Co. Donegal Air

Paddy's Rambles ... (A)

Inspired by a wailing spirit, or banshee, and learned from his grandmother by the great fiddler John Doherty (*c.*1895–1980). Fiddles predominate over all other instruments in the music of the counties of Donegal and Tyrone and the technical level of players like the travelling Doherty family was very high. Note the use of second position in bars A6 and 7.

28

Air du comté de Donegal

Paddy's Rambles ... (*la*)

Cette pièce est inspirée par une forme de lamentation, ou *banshee.* Le grand violoniste John Doherty (*ca* 1895–1980) l'a apprise auprès de sa grand-mère. Le violon traditionnel domine tous les autres instruments dans la musique des comtés de Donegal et de Tyrone et le niveau technique d'interprètes tels que les membres itinérants de la famille Doherty était très haut. Observez l'utilisation de la deuxième position dans les mesures A6 et 7.

28

Air aus der Grafschaft Donegal

Paddy's Rambles ... (A)

Inspiriert durch einen klagenden Geist, oder eine Todesfee, lernte der große Fiddler John Doherty (ca. 1895–1980) diese Weise von seiner Großmutter. In der Musik der Grafschaften Donegal und Tyrone haben die Fiddlen die absolute Vorrangstellung vor allen anderen Instrumenten, und das technische Können z.B. der umherziehenden Spielerfamilie Doherty war sehr hoch. Man beachte den Gebrauch der zweiten Lage in den Takten A6 und 7.

Paddy's Rambles through the Park

29

29

Donegal Germans

Róise Bheag Róise Móire's (D)
Francie Mooney's (D)

Francie Mooney (Proinnsias Ó Maonaigh' in Irish, pronounced *Prawnshuss O'Mweeney*), born in an Irish-speaking area of Donegal, learned many tunes from his mother, Róise Bheag Róise Móire (pronounced *Rosh-er Vyug Rosh-er Mor-a)*. His daughter, Mairéad Mooney, sings and plays fiddle in the famous Donegal band *Altan*.

29

Allemandes (Germans) de Donegal

Róise Bheag Róise Móire's *(ré)*
Francie Mooney's *(ré)*

Francie Mooney ('Proinnsias O Maonaigh' en irlandais), née dans une partie de Donegal où l'on parlais la langue irlandaise, apprit de nombreux airs de sa mère, Roise Bheag Roise Moire. Sa fille, Mairéad Mooney, chante et joue du violon traditionnel dans le fameux ensemble *Altan* de Donegal.

29

Germans aus Donegal

Róise Bheag Róise Móire's (D)
Francie Mooney's (D)

Francie Mooney (im Irischen heißt er „Proinnsais ó Maonaigh", was ungefähr *Proanschass O Muienie* ausgesprochen wird), der in einer irischsprachigen Gegend von Donegal geboren wurde, lernte viele Lieder von seiner Mutter Róise Bheag Róise Móire (ungefähr ausgesprochen als *Rosch-er Wiag Rosch-er Mor-a)*. Seine Tochter Mairéad Mooney singt und fiddlet in der berühmten Band *Altan* aus Donegal.

Róise Bheag Róise Móire's

Francie Mooney's

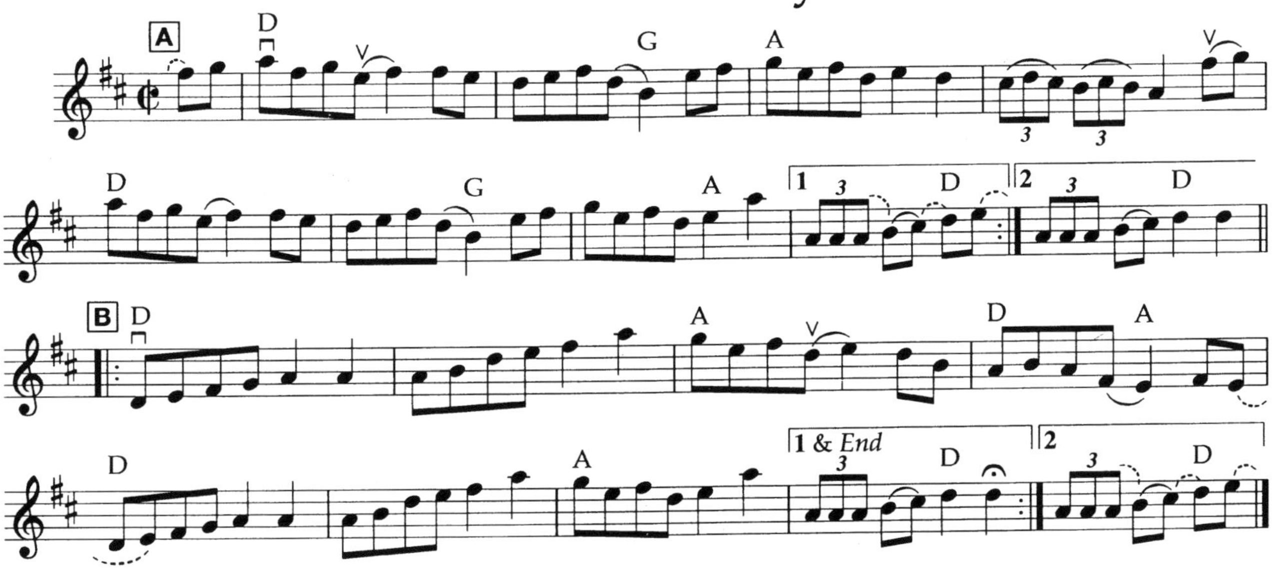

30

30

Donegal Reels

Boys of Malin (A)

The Gravel Walks (A-dorian)

Dinkey's Reel (A-mixolydian)

'There is only a paper wall between Irish and Scottish music', John Doherty once remarked. These reels certainly have a strong Scottish flavour. Malin Head is Ireland's most northerly point. *The Gravel Walks*, from south-west Donegal, is a great tune to 'reverse', or play an octave lower than written. *Dinkey's*, from Mickey and Francie Byrne of Kilcar, celebrates a local footballer and step-dancer.

30

Reels de Donegal

Boys of Malin (*la*)

The Gravel Walks (*la* dorien)

Dinkey's Reel (*la* mixolydien)

«Il n'y qu'un mur de papier entre la musique irlandaise et la musique écossaise» remarqua un jour John Doherty. Ces *reels* sont marqués d'une forte empreinte écossaise. Malin Head est le point le plus septentrional de l'Irlande. *The Gravel Walks*, originaire du sud-est Donegal, est un air superbe à «renverser», ou jouer une octave plus grave que ce qui écrit. *Dinkey's* dû à Mickey et Francie Byrne de Kilcar, célèbre un footballer et *step-dancer* local.

30

Donegal Reels

Boys of Malin (A)

The Gravel Walks (A-dorisch)

Dinkey's Reel (A-mixolydisch)

„Es gibt nur eine Papierwand zwischen irischer und schottischer Musik", bemerkte John Doherty einmal. Diese Reels haben sicherlich eine starke schottische Färbung. Malin Head ist Irlands nördlichster Punkt. *The Gravel Walks*, aus dem Südwesten Donegals, ist ein Lied, das hervorragend zum „Umdrehen" geeignet ist, oder um es eine Oktave tiefer zu spielen als es steht. *Dinkey's Reel*, komponiert von Mickey und Francie Byrne aus Kilcar, feiert einen lokalen Fußballspieler und Stepptänzer.

Boys of Malin

The Gravel Walks

Dinkey's Reel

31

31

Donegal Reels

The Oak Tree (D)
The Flogging Reel (G)
The Glory Reel (G)

I learned the first of these, also called *Na Saighneáin* or *The Northern Lights,* from Donegal-born Tommy Peoples (1948–), perhaps the greatest living Irish fiddler. *The Flogging Reel* may have originated in Scotland, where it is known as the *Flagon Reel. The Glory Reel* comes from the playing of James Byrne. I make no attempt to reproduce the striking one-stroke-per-note bowing favoured by some Donegal players.

31

Reels de Donegal

The Oak Tree *(ré)*
The Flogging Reel *(sol)*
The Glory Reel *(sol)*

J'ai recueilli le premier de ces *reels,* également intitulé *Na Saighneáin* (Les lumières du Nord), auprès de Tommy Peoples, né en 1948 à Donegal, sans doute le plus grand violoniste irlandais vivant. *The Flogging Reel* provient peut-etre d'Ecosse où il est connu sous le nom de *Flagon Reel. The Glory Reel* m'a été transmis par l'interprétation de James Byrne. Je n'ai pas essayé de reproduire l'impressionnant 'un coup d'archet par note' pratiqué par certains interprètes de Donegal.

31

Donegal Reels

The Oak Tree (D)
The Flogging Reel (G)
The Glory Reel (G)

Den ersten der hier vorliegenden Reels, auch *Na Saighneáin* oder *The Northern Lights* gennant, lernte ich von dem in Donegal geborenene Tommy Peoples (*1948), dem vielleicht größten lebenden irischen Fiedler. *The Flogging Reel* könnte seinen Ursprung auch in Schottland haben, wo er unter dem Namen *The Flagon Reel* bekannt ist. *The Glory Reel* stammt von dem Spiel James Byrnes. Ich mache allerdings keinen Versuch, die eindrucksvolle *ein-Strich-pro-Note-*Strichart nachzuahmen, die einige der Spieler aus Donegal bevorzugen.

The Oak Tree

The Flogging Reel

The Glory Reel

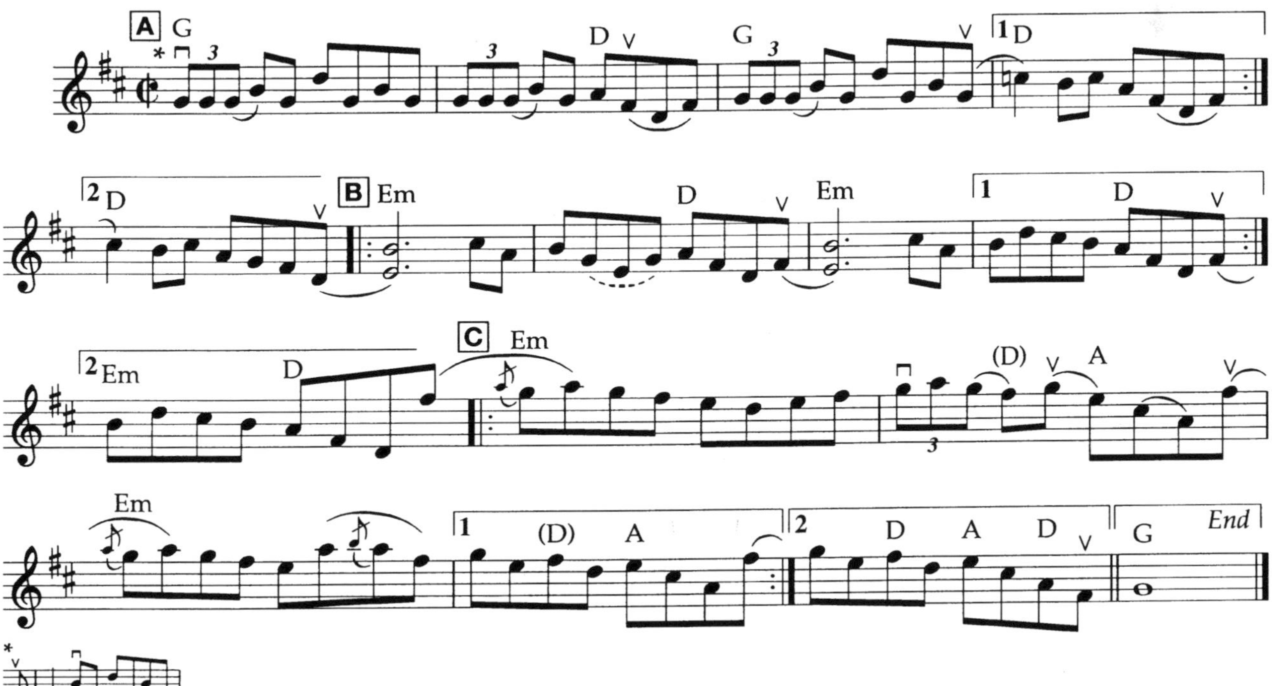

32

32
Air
Coming Home (E-dorian)

We conclude this musical journey with a tune I wrote for a TV film of the same title (director, Moira Sweeney, 1994), and dedicated to friends in Northern Ireland.

32
Air
Coming Home (*mi* dorien)

Nous refermons ce parcours musical par un air que j'ai écrit pour un téléfilm portant le même titre (réalisation Moira Sweeney, 1994) et que j'ai dédié à des amis d'Irlande du Nord.

32
Air
Coming Home (E-dorisch)

Wir beschließen diese musikalische Reise mit einem Lied, das ich für einem TV-Film mit demselben Titel schrieb (1994, die Regisseurin war Moira Sweeney) und Freunden in Nordirland widmete.

Coming Home

Pete Cooper
1994

Further Listening

Some of these recordings, with versions of tunes in this book, may have been deleted, or re-issued on different labels. The entries are listed alphabetically according to the artist's name. Search the internet for latest information.

Discographie - écoute

Enregistrements comportant différentes versions des airs transcripts dans ce recueil, par ordre alphabétique du nom de l'artiste. Consultez également l'Internet – certains titres ont peut-être été réédités par d'autres éditeurs.

Hörempfehlungen

Im Folgenden werden Aufnahmen mit Versionen von Titeln aus diesem Buch aufgeführt. Sie sind alphabetisch nach den Nachnamen der Künstler geordnet. Man durchsuche aber bitte auch das Internet – einige Titel können eventuell von anderen Labels neu herausgegeben worden sein.

The Bothy Band
The First Album (Green Linnet, 1975)
The Coach ('Tar') Road to Sligo,
Coleman's Cross,
Martin Wynne's No. 2,
Craig's Pipes

The Bothy Band
Out of the Wind,
Martin Wynne's No. 1

James Byrne
The Road to Glenlough (Claddagh CC52CD),
The Glory Reel

Liz Carroll
Lost in the Loop (Green Linnet GLCD 1199),
The Flogging Reel

Bobby Casey
Casey in the Cowhouse (Bellbridge Records 001),
Farewell to Miltown

Nollaig Casey & Arty McGlynn
Lead the Knave (MCGLP1)
Lament for Owen Roe O'Neill ('Caoineadh Eoghain Rua'),
Music in the Wind ('Brady's Set'),
Michael O'Connor ('Michael Ward')

Máire ní Chathasaigh & Chris Newman
The Carolan Albums (Old Bridge Music OBMCD06),
The Princess Royal,
Fanny Power

Michael Coleman (1891-1945) (Viva Voce 004),
Farrell O'Gara,
Humours of Ennistymon,
Green Fields of Ros Beigh ('The Kerry Reel')

Matt Cranitch
Éistigh Seal (Gael Linn CEFC104),
Lament for Owen Roe O'Neill
('Caoineadh Eoghain Rua'),
O'Donnell's Lament

Seamus Creagh
Came the Dawn (Ossian OSS CD90),
Julia Clifford's,
Sean Healy's,
Star of Munster

John Doherty
The Floating Bow (Claddagh CCF31CD),
The Flogging Reel

John Doherty
Bundle and Go (Topic 12TS39),
Paddy's Rambles through the Park

Luch Farr
Heart and Home (Veteran V12),
Andy Davy's,
The Pullet & the Cock

Paddy Glackin
In Full Spate (Gael Linn CEFCD153),
Paddy's Rambles Through The Park

Martin Hayes
Under the Moon (Green Linnet GLCD 115),
Galway Bay,
Kilfenora Jig,
Cliffs of Moher,
Farewell to Miltown

Paddy Killoran
Back in Town (Shanachie 33003),
Sligo Maid (' 's Lament')

The London Lasses
Track Across the Deep (LL002-A),
Fig For A Kiss

Andy McGann & Paul Brady
It's a Hard Road to Travel (Shanachie 29009)
Galway Bay

James Morrison
The Professor (Viva Voce 001),
The Wandering Minstrel

Denis Murhpy and Julia Clifford
The Star Above the Garter
(Claddagh Records CC5CD),
Dan O'Donnell's Lament O'Keeffe's Slides

Eilish O'Connor
Sugrá (TODCD 200),
The Dusty Miller

Pádraig O'Keeffe
The Sliabh Luachra
Fiddle Master (RTÉ CD174)
O'Donnell's Lament

Tommy Peoples
The High Part Of the Road
(Shanachie SH29003)
The Oak Tree,
O'Farrell's Welcome To Limerick

Tommy Peoples
The Iron Man (Shanachie SH79044),
Tom Billy's

Brian Rooney
The Godfather (Racket Records RR CD002)
The Wandering Minstrel,
The Sligo Maid

Joe Ryan
An Buachaill Dreoite (Cló Iar CICD 113),
Martin Wynne's No.1
The Princess Royal,
The Coolin

Slibh Notes
Gleanntán (Ossian OSS CD114),
Nell O'Sullivan's,
Gullane Polka

Various
Fiddlesticks, Music
from Donegal (Nimbus Records NI 5320)
The Boys of Malin,
The Gravel Walks,
Fergal ('Farrell') O'Gara

Various
The Donegal Fiddle (RTÉ 196),
Dinkey's ('Dinkey Dorrian's Reel),
The Glory Reel ('Ríl na nGlór'),
The ('Old') Oak Tree

Various
The Fiddle Music
of Donegal (Cairdeas CNF001),
Róise Bheag Róise Móire's,
Francie Mooney's,
Fergal ('Feargal') O'Gara

Pete Cooper's website:
www.petecooper.com

Index of Pieces by Dance Type
(in alphabetical order)

See Contents for listing of pieces in order of performance on the CD

Index des pièces par types de danses
(en ordre alphabétique)

Voir dans le Sommaire la liste des pièces dans l'ordre de leur exécution sur le CD

Werktitel nach Tanztyp
(alphabetisch geordnet)

Für die Reihenfolge der Stücke auf die CD siehe das Inhaltsverzeichnis

Reels

Andy Davy's (track 14, p. 30)
Boys of Malin (track 30, p. 50)
The Christmas Eve (track 27, p. 46)
Craig's Pipes (track 27, p. 47)
Dinkey's Reel (track 30, p. 51)
Farewell To Miltown (track 11, p. 27)
Fergal O'Gara (track 8, p. 23)
Fermoy Lasses (track 27, p. 47)
The Flogging Reel (track 31, p. 53)
The Glory Reel (track 31, p. 53)
The Gravel Walks (track 30, p. 50)
Green Fields Of Ros Beigh (track 8, p. 23)
Martin Wynne's No. 1 (track 23, p. 40)
- No. 2 (track 23, p. 40)
- No. 3 (track 23, p. 41)
The Oak Tree (track 31, p. 52)
Over the Moor to Maggie (track 24, p. 43)
The Porthole of the Kelp (track 11, p. 27)
The Pullet & The Cock (track 14, p. 30)
The Sligo Maid (track 26, p. 44)
The Star of Munster (track 26, p. 45)
Swinging on the Gate (track 25, p. 42)

Double Jigs

The Bank of Turf (track 3, p. 17)
The Cliffs of Moher (track 9, p. 25)
The Coach Road to Sligo (track 22, p. 38)
Coleman's Cross (track 22, p. 39)
Donnybrook Fair (track 21, p. 37)
Kilfenora Jig (track 9, p. 25)
Humours of Ennistymon (track 9, p. 24)
Tom Billy's Favourite (track 3, p. 17)
The Trip to Sligo (track 22, p. 39)
The Wandering Minstrel (track 21, p. 37)

Slip Jigs

A Fig for a Kiss (track 20, p. 35)
The Dusty Miller (track 20, p. 35)
O'Farrell's Welcome To Limerick (track 21, p. 36)

Single Jigs and Slides

Dan O'Keeffe's Nr. 1 (track 4, p. 19)
Dan O'Keeffe's Nr. 2 (track 4, p. 19)
The Lonesome Jig (track 15, p. 31)
Music On The Wind (track 15, p. 31)
Nell O'Sullivan's (track 5, p. 20)
Scully Casey's (track 4, p. 18)

Hornpipes

Galway Bay Hornpipe (track 16, p. 32)
The Home Brew (track 16, p. 32)
Julia Clifford's (track 2, p. 16)
McGivney's Hornpipe (track 12, p. 28)
The Plains of Boyle (track 12, p. 28)
Sean Healey's (track 2, p. 16)

Airs

Lament For Owen Roe O'Neill (track 10, p. 26)
Coming Home (track 32, p. 54)
The Coulin (track 24, p. 42)
Fanny Power (track 19, p. 34)
Lament For O'Donnell (track 1, p. 15)
Michael O'Connor (track 17, p. 33)
Paddy's Rambles Through The Park (track 28, p. 48)
The Princess Royal (track 18, p. 34)

Polkas

Ballydesmond Polka Nr. 3 (track 7, p. 22)
Ballyhoura Mountains (track 13, p. 29)
The Gullane Polka (track 5, p. 20)
Knocknaboul Polka (track 7, p. 22)
Lucy Farr's Polka (track 13, p. 29)
Toormore Polka Nr. 1 (track 6, p. 21)
Toormore Polka Nr. 2 (track 6, p. 21)

Germans

Francie Mooney's (track 29, p. 49)
Róise Bheag Róise Móire's (track 29, p. 49)

All pieces performed by Pete Cooper
Recorded and Mastered by Jon Wilkinson